Misperceptions of Economic Phenomena

F. E. Brown
Professor of Marketing and Statistics
Wharton School, University of Pennsylvania

and

A. R. Oxenfeldt
Professor of Marketing
Graduate School of Business
Columbia University

Sperr & Douth, Inc.
New York, New York

348848

HC
110
.C6B75
1972

CONTENTS

PREFACE

A preface should mainly tell the reader something about the book and warn him of the authors' biases. We shall try to do both.

We believe that economic misperceptions as a general phenomenon shared by most individuals are common to all phases of economic life. However, we find that individuals do differ in perceptual accuracy; and, the general accuracy of perception varies according to the economic phenomenon considered. We see both the magnitude of these misperceptions and the losses they cause as substantial. Finally, we do not believe these points are widely recognized and taken into account by executives.

We did not start the project reported in this book with the views stated in the preceding paragraph. Indeed, we did not start out to study economic misperceptions. Our project began as a study of perceptions of food prices by the different parties involved: The ultimate customer, the retailer, the supplier, government agencies, trading stamp companies, the advertising agencies and different individuals within each organization. The project changed focus and direction as we played ideas, alternative approaches, and related applications back and forth to each other (and to anyone else who would listen). We found the same sorts of questions arising over and over. What does it mean if perceptions are inaccurate? What factors might produce inaccuracy? What could or should various participants do if their perceptions are inaccurate? if perceptions by other participants are inaccurate? How is this situation similar to other economic situations? How is it different?

The temptation to get on with the empirical work, both data collection and analysis, was great. Had we moved more rapidly, the generality of economic misperceptions might have been missed while the empirical content of our findings might have been more utilitarian. We wish our data were more current, but we do believe the orders of magnitude we found still hold.

Our empirical work deals almost exclusively with food store prices and stresses the accuracy or inaccuracy of the shopper's perceptions. We no longer view price perceptions as an end in themselves; rather, their value derives from the light they cast on the incidence and forms of economic misperceptions. Increasingly, we are considering the potential relevance and transferability of our findings to labor markets, education, and investments. Other areas of economic activity afflicted with substantial misperception will no doubt occur to many readers.

The empirical work reported here also illustrates a general methodology that is appropriate for most studies of economic misperceptions. The measurement problems of both perception and reality are addressed, and alternative ways of expressing the accuracy of perception are considered. These questions are far from trivial, and we trust that our attempts to cope with them will assist others who study misperception.

Finally, our empirical work forced us to answer again and again two questions. "How is the perception used in decision-making?" and "What are the likely causes of misperceptions?" The first led us to examine perceptions only in the light of particular decisions. We believe that perceptual validity has little social significance outside a decision-specific context. The second led us to consider and include within the book a brief discussion of a psychological model of perception as it relates to economic misperceptions.

Completion of this project was made possible by the assistance of many persons. Principal acknowledgement must go to Marge Brown and to the Sperry and Hutchinson Research Committee. Mrs. Brown typed every draft of the manuscript and all of the articles resulting from the project. She served not only as typist but as discerning critic and editor. The Sperry and Hutchinson Research Committee financed the project and offered valuable advice and comments. But at no time did it seek to override the authors. Dr. Eugene R. Beem, Mr. Jay Shaffer, and Mr. Larry Isaacson of the Sperry and Hutchinson Company were particularly helpful in their comments, both on substantive and methodological points.

Dr. Richard L. Wendell, now of the University of Connecticut, bore the brunt of the field supervision, spending long hours and editing countless forms—tasks for which we are deeply grateful. Dr. Roger A.

Diskinson, now of Rutgers University, supervised the field work in San Francisco, permitting additional geographic spread for the project.

Mr. Shepley W. Evans and Mr. Irwin D. Reid served as research assistants while students at the University of Pennsylvania. They both contributed greatly in the analytic phase, overseeing data processing and adding helpful suggestions in making concepts operational. Mr. Charles Turner, a student at Columbia University, was our chief guide in searching the psychological literature on perception.

Work done by the Department of Agriculture in a one-year pricing study in Greensboro gave us valuable insights prior to going into the field. Mr. John Galvin and Rosalind Lifquist were extremely helpful and informative; Dr. Paul Nelson raised theoretical points that we may have otherwise missed.

Dr. Anthony G. Kelly, Mr. Carl Nelson, and Mr. Anees Hussain, while students at Columbia University, evaluated the definitions of perceptual validity. Dr. Charles S. Goodman, University of Pennsylvania, and Dr. Robert Rothberg, Rutgers University, gave valuable guidance in the pre-testing of data collection instruments. Mr. William Alrich, Editor of the Wharton Quarterly, read the original manuscript and offered many helpful suggestions concerning revisions. The pricers and interviewers, of course, collected the data. Without them, there would be no empirical content and no documentation for any of our generalization. The authors, of course, accept responsibility for all errors of commission and omission.

Part I

Introduction
and Method

Economic decisions are based upon the perceptions of particular problem situations, but these perceptions rarely coincide with reality. Part I explores the pervasiveness of economic misperception, the importance and probable consequences of it, and some of the problems in its study. First, the general subject is sketched with particular emphasis on its possible ramifications for individual and social welfare. The discussion then focuses on *buyer* perception, identifying important dimensions of purchase transactions. Part I concludes with the presentation of the research design for the empirical content of this study.

Chapter I

MISPERCEPTIONS OF ECONOMIC PHENOMENA: HOW MUCH? WHY? SO WHAT?

Economic and market analyses rely very heavily on the "facts" of the situation. Lip service is paid to the importance of image and anticipations, but the analyst often shifts to an investigation of what is "really" being offered or what the consumer is "really" doing. Frequently the shift occurs without recognition that a shift from images to reality has taken place.

This report asserts that (1) many people do not perceive economic phenomena accurately and (2) their behavior is explained better by their perceptions than by reality. The principal basis for our report is a large-scale empirical study of housewives' perceptions of food prices. The results are of substantive significance in themselves, but they also illustrate a method for studying other misperceptions.

To make a comprehensive analysis of economic misperceptions, we need to study many different *participants* in the economic process and many different *phenomena* that each participant must perceive. The following suggestive catalog of the participants and phenomena will indicate the scope and contents of the domain of economic perceptions. Foremost among the parties to the economic process in the United States are: buyers, sellers, employers, employees, producers, consumers, suppliers, investors, advertisers, and government regulators. There is no reason to believe that these groups are equally susceptible to misperceptions or that their misperceptions are of equal economic significance. But each group is sufficiently important to warrant study of its misperceptions.

Each participant in the economic order is concerned with particular phenomena and processes. For example, a shopper is mainly affected by the prices charged by different sources of supply, the quality of competing products, service available, reliability of the supplier, and breadth of assortment. The seller, on the other hand, is concerned with the wishes of his potential customers. Do they favor him more or less than before, and why is this true? Clearly, actions by buyers and sellers are influenced by their perceptions. These perceptions lead to actions that determine the realization of individual goals and the success with which the economy uses resources.

Investors are concerned with demands for products in the future, potential cost savings, the cost of acquiring plant and facilities, and the technological reliability of different productive processes—matters of only minor concern to most buyers and sellers of goods. Laborers likewise have special concerns: such as the rates of pay available from different occupations and at individual firms, the opportunities for advancement provided by each accessible employer, the pleasantness of working conditions, the form and degree of fringe benefits. Therefore, substantial misperceptions by investors and laborers will influence their behavior and will result in decisions that reduce both their own economic well-being and general economic efficiency.

The catalog could continue indefinitely, but the direction should now be clear. Any comprehensive investigation of misperceptions in the economy must consider the large number of participants whose perceptions influence the economic behavior and efficiency as well as the phenomena they perceive. This subject is vast and intricate; at most, our report represents a start toward the assembly of the enormous body of information needed to illuminate this dark corner of economic knowledge. It presents a method for investigating the subject of misperceptions and suggests the potential dimensions and implications of the problems such misperceptions create.

THE IMPORTANCE OF ECONOMIC MISPERCEPTIONS

Misperceptions are accorded considerable importance in most branches of social science but are virtually ignored by economists. The whole field of attitude change revolves about individuality. Different individuals evaluate and react to reality situations in highly diverse ways. They also respond in dissimilar ways to changes in reality situations and in communications about reality changes. Psychoanalysis and psychotherapy largely have as their goal the reduction of misperceptions of self, of others, and of the environment. The presence, incidence, magnitude, and effects of misperceptions in the economic sphere would warrant study even if existing evidence did not suggest that they might be substantial. But every study of market phenomena such as buyers' evaluations of relative price, quality, and service shows that many individuals hold conflicting views of the same set of facts.

A second reason for investigating the misperception of economic phenomena is the great effort devoted in the United States to the creation of economic misperceptions. Even as most individuals try to persuade others that they are more intelligent, important, admired, successful, prosperous, and cultivated than they really are, so too vendors, employers, and borrowers try to "puff" their own attractiveness in ways that will serve their self-interest. We may criticize the efforts by marketing specialists to create unjustifiably favorable perceptions of their offerings. However, similar efforts are made by other participants in the economic process but pass largely without comment. With such great effort and so many resources devoted to the creation of misperceptions, we must wonder whether and to what extent these efforts bear fruit. And, if they do, we should not ignore their effects.

To assess the importance of misperceptions in the economic sphere, we must answer several subsidiary questions.

—Are misperceptions confined to a small group, or are they spread over a substantial number of participants? If a small group, who belongs to that group?

—Are misperceptions large or small in size?

—Are the effects of misperceptions trivial or serious in their social significance?

As we indicate in the following chapters, many buyers misperceive the prices of food to a substantial degree. Other evidence—notably the data assembled by Consumers Union over the last 35 years—also suggests that buyers' perceptions of quality depart substantially from reality. Beyond the present state of affairs, the growing dynamism and complexity of the economy will increase the difficulty of forming valid perceptions.

The economic effects of misperceptions pose very complex questions. We see three main standpoints from which the significance of misperceptions should be viewed:

(1) The welfare of the individual participants.

(2) The efficiency with which the chief economic mechanisms operate in the presence of substantial misperceptions.

(3) The explanation and prediction of economic phenomena by economic and marketing specialists.

Welfare of Individual Participants

Persons who do not perceive accurately the number and nature of the alternatives available to them are likely to make sub-optimal decisions whether they are buyers, investors, or laborers. In some cases, their choices might result in personal injury or suffering. They surely would not obtain as much satisfaction from actions based on misperceptions as they could obtain from actions based on valid perceptions. Quite simply, individuals must perceive accurately in order to maximize their satisfactions.

Individuals *do not* receive additional satisfaction when the alternative they select is better than initially perceived.'The effect of the misperception hinges on the decision that is reached. Misperception cannot lead to a correct decision; it can only mislead. If the individual makes a correct decision despite the misperception, he does not receive additional benefit *because* of the misperception.

One can easily agree with the foregoing generalizations and still attach only slight significance to economic misperceptions. If misperceptions are small, occur only occasionally, and represent phenomena that have minor bearing on individual welfare, they might safely be ignored in analyses of the economy. Since we cannot assume misperceptions to be small and occasional, the purpose of this study is to cast light on their magnitude and importance.

One could hope that whatever misperceptions do occur are concentrated among those individuals who can most easily bear their cost. Here again, we have little reason to comfort ourselves. The folklore and the limited evidence available suggest that misperceptions are most prevalent among the uneducated, insecure, inexperienced— those who are economically disadvantaged and would continue to be disadvantaged even if they were to act on the basis of perfect perceptions.

Efficiency of Basic Economic Mechanisms

The efficiency of our economy is measured by the way it allocates available resources in meeting the population's needs. The effects of misperceptions on this allocation process will show their influence on overall social activity. We must therefore ask whether markets will behave well or poorly if a substantial number of buyers, sellers, investors, employees, and employers misperceive the relevant economic realities.

The "rational man" of economic theory is assumed to be aware of all changes in the market place and to know its true state. Misperceptions represent a departure from this basic assumption, and we see them as a possible cause of malfunction in the market mechanism. Two arguments have been raised against this conclusion, and they deserve examination. (1) Buyer misperceptions are offsetting and therefore do not impair the workings of market mechanisms. (2) The forces of competition protect against malfunctioning that might otherwise result from misperception.

Will efficient markets result if buyers' errors in perception are offsetting? It has been argued that market participants need not perceive market phenomena accurately; rather, the market mechanism will perform efficiently if perceptual errors are offsetting.[1] This line of argument is ordinarily accompanied by the assertion that there is no strong reason to expect perceptual errors to be biased in one direction so that they probably are distributed in a symmetrical fashion and are offsetting. Let us examine this argument closely.

First, if half the buyers greatly exaggerate the value of a particular offering and the other half underestimate its value by an equal amount, both groups will make mistaken decisions and presumably suffer some waste of their resources. Their errors will not offset each other in terms of the satisfaction that the individuals derive from their purchases. Misperceptions will result in a decrease of social welfare (the sum of individual welfares) as well as a decrease in personal welfare. Even if the efficiency of the market mechanism were not adversely affected by misperceptions, public welfare is injured by misperception.

Exactly offsetting perceptual errors could produce the same distribution of patronage among stores and brands that would result

---

[1] Exactly offsetting errors can be defined in various ways. For example, they could be said to occur when the number of customers who avoid one store because they exaggerate its expensiveness is equal to the number who patronize it because they underestimate its expensiveness; or, when an equal number of units are not purchased by some and are purchased by others because of mistaken perceptions of price. In one case, the number of customers would be the same as it would be if perceptions were completely accurate. In the other case, the number of units purchased would be the same. Misperceptions could also be considered offsetting when price distortion—without regard to behavior—is distributed symmetrically around reality.

from accurate perceptions. We might suppose that, in such a situation, the discipline of the market would have the desired effect on vendors. That view is questionable because misperceptions probably obscure the bases for market discipline. They blur the connection between the sellers' actions and their consequences. As a result, sellers may not learn for a long time, if ever, what factors make for success or how to please their customers. One well-established conclusion from learning theory is that consistent reinforcement greatly facilitates the learning process. On balance, we conclude that efficiency of the market mechanism is injured even when perceptual errors are offsetting.

Explanations of market behavior must account for more than market totals. They must explain the separate parts of the market. Each market is composed of many segments. Most segments pursue their own interests but ultimately fail because of misperceptions. An understanding of the market would require a knowledge of the factors making for misperceptions, a knowledge of the reasons why the individual segments misperceive in the way they do, and an analysis of the consequences of misperceptions for each group of buyers and for the firms that sell to them. Exactly offsetting misperceptions would in no way obviate the need for perceptual studies by those who want to explain market phenomena.

We would hardly expect exactly offsetting misperceptions. The reverse is more likely. The forces making for individual misperceptions would be expected to affect many individuals in the same way, thus creating systematic perceptual biases rather than offsetting errors. These effects may then be contagious and perhaps cumulative. At the very least, the existence or nonexistence of offsetting misperceptions should be investigated—not assumed or theorized away.

A New Explanatory Variable in Market Analysis

Market events explained solely in terms of realities may be ignoring a variable that has considerable explanatory power. "Reality economics" has not been such a powerful analytic tool that we can ignore other promising explanations. Economic theory grew more powerful when "anticipations" were introduced as an explicit variable in analyses of general business conditions. Its introduction made it necessary to consider possible differences in the anticipations of individuals within any group and among groups of economic participants. We propose that perceptions of economic phenomena be introduced as an explicit variable in all economic analyses.

Several examples will suggest the kinds of things that would follow from this proposal. An analyst might find that the unit sales of an item have declined despite a price reduction. Such a phenomenon runs counter to expectations but would be thoroughly understandable if we learned that virtually no customers were aware of the price reduction, or it would be understandable if most customers interpreted (perceived) the lowering of price as evidence that the item was of low quality and not popular. In other words, the item was perceived as less attractive than it had been, and the price change caused the new perception.

Many unexpected and puzzling events may become intelligible when we take into account the failure of the affected market participants to perceive reality accurately. A retailer may be puzzled by the fact that his market share is very small despite the demonstrable fact that his prices are lower and the quality and services offered are higher than those of his rivals. Research might establish that most customers perceive his prices to be relatively high—whatever the facts. And, of course, his own perceptions of prices, quality, and services might be in error and increase his errors in diagnosis.

Potential Significance of Economic Misperceptions

The phenomenon of buyer misperceptions cannot be dismissed as unimportant or "self-correcting." Neither armchair speculation nor the meager evidence available justifies a reliance on "reality economics." On the contrary, the foregoing remarks suggest that we may need a special sub-variety of economics—one that analyzes the perceptual worlds of buyers, laborers, investors, sellers, and others. The purpose of this branch of economics would be to measure perceptions and to investigate the incidence, nature, and effects of misperceptions. Its ultimate objective would be to find remedies for situations in which individuals suffered seriously or the economy performed poorly as a result of misperceptions.

More specifically, "perceptual economics" would have the following objectives:

1. To describe the magnitude of the misperceptions by various participants in economic activity.

2. To indicate phenomena that are commonly misperceived.

3. To explain how major misperceptions come about.

4. To describe and explain which individuals' perceptions are accurate and which individuals' perceptions are inaccurate.

5. To suggest methods of correcting misperceptions that lead to objectionable consequences and to predict the results of such measures.

In addition, we propose that a separate branch of marketing is needed to deal with perceptual phenomena. A substantial portion of the marketing efforts of the nation's largest firms is devoted to creating perceptions favorable to the firms and their products. Typically, these efforts are described as "creating a favorable brand image." Merely recognizing that these efforts involve the perceptual process may improve substantially the quality of studies of image-building. Current marketing discussions shift from reality to perception without recognizing the shift so that both communication and the validity of conclusions drawn are likely to suffer.

Perceptual marketing—if such a sub-branch ever develops—would devote considerable attention to the study of sellers' and resellers' perceptions. Those who attempt to alter the perceptions of others do not necessarily perceive their own situations validly. Our interviews suggest that resellers do not perceive more accurately than most buyers. The poorest perceivers among resellers are better than the poorest perceivers among buyers, but the two groups are very similar with respect to the average level of misperception.

Accordingly, buyer perceptions deserve close study if we are to understand the extent to which buyers meet their own goals and if we are to improve the efficiency of the market mechanism. We also need to compare buyers' abilities to perceive the relevant reality among different products and among different sellers. Finally, we need to compare perceptual abilities of various buyers. But what do we mean by buyer perceptions? And how might we study them?

ECONOMIC PERCEPTIONS DEFINED

Behavioral scientists distinguish a hierarchy of psychological processes ranging from raw sensation through perception to the higher mental processes like creativity. Each of these levels represents different proportions of pure sensation and of mental manipulation. At the sensation end of the spectrum, the brain contributes very little to the result, though some process beyond pure sensation is almost always involved. For example, the brain inverts images that the eyes receive. At the higher mental process end of the spectrum, the brain's contribution may be almost total, as in the case of pure imagination.

While no sharp lines can be drawn between these psychological processes, our objectives do not require such a demarcation. Our chief concern is with the distortion and misinterpretation of reality by participants in economic activity. This apparently takes place in the perceptual process which includes the following:

—The selective process, by which certain market phenomena are selected for "sensing."

—The selective process, by which certain things are remembered accurately, forgotten, or distorted in memory.

—The interpretation or explanation of events—the process by which individuals give meaning to their experience.

—The retrieving and organization of past experience, meaning both the fruits of past learning and the ability to learn.

The definition of perception employed here conforms fairly close to that found in the psychological literature, but it has been adapted to the needs of someone concerned with economic behavior.[2] The definition will become clear if we indicate the phenomena excluded from buyer perceptions. Above all, *simple and crude memory*— unorganized recollections of the past or information about the present that has not been interpreted—*is not perception*. The correct memory of prices charged in the past or knowledge of the prices being charged currently does not represent valid perceptions of price (or invalid perceptions, either). Only if properly interpreted, will such memory and knowledge contribute to valid price perceptions. Similarly, incorrect memories do not constitute invalid perceptions although they may lie at the foundation of invalid price perceptions. We must relate the role of price memories to the focus of our interest: how well buyers meet their own goals and how well the market mechanism operates.

[2] See for example, B. Barelson and G. Steiner, *Human Behavior, An Inventory of Scientific Findings*, New York: Harcourt, Brace, and World, Inc., 1964, p.88. A more detailed model of the perceptual process is presented in Chapter VII.

How much does a buyer gain from correct memory of the prices of the items he has purchased or is about to purchase? Memory of past prices may serve as a jumping off spot for decisions, but it is no more than that. If a buyer remembered that he once paid or that newspapers advertised TV sets of a particular brand and size for, say, $200.00, his inclination to explore the wisdom of making a purchase might be greater than if his recollection was that a set cost $250.00.

His memory alone would be a relatively poor basis for deciding whether to explore the wisdom of such a purchase for several reasons. First, prices do change for any item, even in the same store. Second, prices for the same item may differ substantially at different stores. Third, items frequently change in physical form and in features offered to buyers. Fourth, what we read and hear and remember is necessarily less than all of the information we would desire for the usual buying decision. Indeed, prospective buyers expect information derived from promotional advertising to be less than total and not wholly reliable. If the final price is subject to negotiation, memory might not tell the buyer much about what he could achieve through negotiation and bargaining. That information almost always requires an actual test.

One can define buyer perceptions almost as he wishes. Any definition espoused will not be a departure from other given definitions since virtually no one has been concerned with these questions. However, the foregoing discussion establishes that accurate memory of price is not sufficient for buyers to meet their needs. In order to understand buyer behavior and its consequences, *we must identify and isolate those aspects of buyer psychic activity that contribute to buyer decisions*. Specifically, what should a customer "know," "perceive," "understand,"—the particular words used should not matter—to be an efficient buyer?

Precisely the same kinds of questions must be asked about other economic participants, such as investors, laborers, employers, borrowers, and sellers. When that is done, we discover that a participant in economic activities is concerned with far more than information about the present state of affairs. The participant desires information mainly as a basis for forecasting, for decisions take effect in the future.

To talk about the perceptions of all participants in economic activity and their perceptions of all relevant phenomena is extremely cumbersome. Since the empirical portion of this report is concerned with housewives' perceptions of food prices, we will illustrate the issues involved with *buyers'* perceptions.

Chief Dimensions of Buyer Perceptions

What must a buyer perceive if he is to maximize his welfare? What, beyond knowledge of the prices charged by alternative sources of supply, does he require? Even more specifically, what perceptions will influence an individual buyer's behavior? Apparently, buyers must settle at least the following kinds of questions for themselves:

—Information required. What information might help me, make correct judgments about prospective purchases? What are the relevant factors in choosing among alternatives, including the "no purchase" alternative?

—Value of information. What information is worth collecting? What is the expected magnitude of differences among alternatives? What is the psychic value of the purchase? Is the likelihood of a purchase sufficiently great to justify the time and effort involved in "shopping around?"

—Sources of information. Where should I look to get the information I require to determine whether to make a purchase? That is, in which stores? at whose advertisements? in which media? which individuals should I consult?

—Places of purchase. In which store or stores should I shop in an effort to obtain the best value?

—Time of purchase. When should I make my purchase? Would some delay be advantageous? Must I rush my purchase?

—Quantity of purchase. How much should I purchase? Should I stock up? Should I buy a minimum in the expectation of being able to buy cheaper (or to get a superior product) at a later time?

—Distribution of purchases. In how many different stores should I shop? Is there a great deal of variability in the different offerings of the same store, or is a single store uniformly superior in all offerings?

The foregoing may not be all of the questions that a buyer must answer to meet his needs. The questions will vary somewhat with the different kinds of things he buys and the different roles he might occupy. The needs and resulting questions of a purchasing agent for a large firm will differ from those of a young child buying a piece of confectionary. Nevertheless, this list does establish several central points. First, it shows that the buyer's concern with "knowing" is related to several different types of action. Different decisions require different types of information. Second, substantive knowledge of the specific buying situation is required before we can select the aspects of perception most deserving of study. Third, it is wise to define buyer perception so that it revolves around those issues germane to buyer behavior. This includes the buyer's predictions of future conditions as well as his knowledge of the present or past.

If we accept these conclusions, we shift from defining perceptions as memory or information (which are both nevertheless involved) to quite different things. In order to identify relevant economic perceptions, we must list the decisions and actions required of economic participants and the perceptions, information, and understanding that they will find helpful in reaching these decisions.

RELEVANT BUYER PERCEPTIONS

Buyers consciously seek many benefits from every purchase. Moreover, a rational buyer would attach importance to many dimensions of offerings beyond price. Let us examine the more important of these dimensions, without attempting to be all-inclusive. This examination should show the varied market aspects that buyers must know or understand if they are to perceive these dimensions accurately. Also, it should suggest which of these dimensions is likely to be most important for most buyers—*most* buyers, rather than buyers in general or all buyers, because buyers differ in the importance they assign to individual dimensions.[3]

It is useful to separate the dimensions of an offering into two major classes. The first concerns the item itself; the second class

---

[3]The importance of a particular dimension should not be confused with the amount of variation among alternatives in this dimension. A buyer may consider the particular dimension important but perceive no differences among alternatives with respect to that dimension. Since the dimension is important to him, he must first form perceptions concerning variability among alternatives even though the dimension is not used as a basis for choice in this particular instance.

concerns the sellers from whom the item might be obtained. Both of these factors involve a large number of sub-factors.

Product Dimensions

Products are as different as people. If we consider all products, we can compose a very long list of product dimensions that are sometimes vital to buyers. The following list is only partial, but suggests a large number of things that most buyers consider relevant in selecting among alternative brands and products.

-Substantive performance of the product—how well it does the job for which it was designed;

-Durability—the length of time that the product can be made to serve before replacement;

-Reliability—the freedom of the product from breakdown;

-Aesthetic appeal;

-Uniqueness;

-Protection against loss—guarantees, warranties, and return privileges offered by the producer—which permits the buyer to avoid serious penalties if purchase proves to be a mistake;

-Convenience in use—the ease with which the product may be stored, moved, shipped, and used;

-Impressions that the ownership of the item makes on others—social status, an appearance of affluence.

It would be an error to regard all these factors as a single phenomenon. Each is a separate dimension of a product; buyers may be able to perceive some with high accuracy while they misperceive others badly.

Substantial differences exist in buyer tastes with respect to most of these dimensions. What is aesthetically pleasing to some may offend others; what some consider a high level of performance may be unacceptable to others. We do not expect much difference among buyers in their definitions of durability and reliability, though the emphasis that individual buyers place on these attributes will vary.

Consequently, reality varies among buyers. Both the relative importance of the various dimensions and the definitions of those dimensions differ from one buyer to another. If we wish to measure the validity of buyer perceptions, we must admit that individual buyers should try to perceive accurately different aspects of an offering. Buyers should be concerned mainly with those attributes that they prize highly or dislike most. Inasmuch as buyers place different values on individual attributes, they should also try to perceive different things; presumably, their perceptual skills should be judged by the validity or accuracy of different kinds of perception.

Dimensions of the Seller

When a product is purchased through an intermediary, the buyer establishes a relationship with both the producer of the product and with the reseller from whom he makes his purchase. Both ordinarily will affect the benefits he achieves from his purchases. What dimensions of the vendor are of importance to buyers in the usual situation?

Buyers report the following aspects of vendors as of primary importance, the relative rank varying from product to product and from person to person.

—The breadth of assortment that the vendor offers.

—The services that the seller renders—including such things as delivery, wrapping, provision of credit, parking, and check cashing.

—Ease of shopping—convenient location, attractiveness of vendor's premises, and merchandise displays.

—Personal relationship with the vendor, salesmen, and/or the management of the enterprise.

To appraise all of these and other attributes, the buyer must obtain considerable sensory information and interpret that information through processes we describe as perception and cognition. The validity with which he perceives these attributes of a vendor will affect the level of satisfaction he derives from his purchases.[4]

[4]It is possible to exaggerate the gains from precise perceptions; the foregoing line of argument should not be interpreted to mean that any departure from precision involves serious losses of satisfaction. We acknowledge that "satisfaction" is a subjective state and can be accompanied by feelings of elation not justified by reality. However, we would expect most mistakes to be recognized ultimately. When they are recognized, the person who erred because of his misperceptions suffers both the realistic loss from having made a mistaken selection and from awareness that he committed an error.

Many customers do not buy products; they "buy a store." That is, they patronize particular stores for each major class of product, without investigating competing alternatives in other stores. Accordingly, the perceptions of buyers that matter most in explaining the distribution of patronage for individual items relate to their evaluations of stores. An analysis of which store characteristics foster valid perceptions by customers is, therefore, of great importance. Which factors tend to give stores better "images" than they deserve, and which factors cause stores to be valued less than the facts warrant? Information about the proportion of stores that are perceived validly, that enjoy better reputations than they deserve, and that are undervalued is sorely lacking. It would be of extreme interest and commercial value to be able to explain those misperceptions.

Which Market Attributes Must Be Perceived Validly

Since products vary so widely and buyers are also very dissimilar, we cannot reach broad generalizations concerning which attributes of an offering are most important. This conclusion is quite significant in itself. It argues against the widespread assumption that buyers should concern themselves primarily with price relative to quality. It calls for analyses of the market process which take account of all important dimensions. Once we consider the total market process, we find many surprises in the ranking that different buyers assign to various factors. For example, it appears that modest differences in price matter very little to the overwhelming majority of customers. Such considerations as convenience seem to matter far more. Convenience, price, and reliability apparently have little influence on the purchase of beauty aids for women, while these factors may dominate the choice for many other purchases. Personal trust and friendliness may matter for a majority of buyers far more than price and convenience in the purchase of services such as haircuts, auto repairs, appliance repairs, and medical care.

The difficulty of forming a valid perception of a particular dimension must not be confused with the importance of the dimension. Buyers' abilities to meet their goals vary with their ability to process large quantities of different kinds of information. Moreover, the ability of individual customers to perceive the various dimensions of a product offering and of vendors is far from uniform. For most buyers and most purchases, price is probably far easier to perceive than quality. Service may be extremely difficult to assess prior to purchase and may be even more difficult to perceive than quality. The ability to perceive these dimensions probably varies from one product group to another, with very large differences among individual buyers in this ability.

SPECIFIC RESEARCH OBJECTIVES

The preceding discussion sketches the framework within which exploratory studies of economic misperceptions can be performed and warns against the temptation to draw broad generalizations. Such exploratory studies are possible for many of the more important participants, market attributes, and for specific dimensions of these attributes. We are probably not ready to measure the overall validity of perceptions at the operational level of broad decision making—such a measurement requires the introduction of a weighting scheme adjusted for each individual's goals. But first steps never yield final answers.

The empirical portion of this report examines the validity of specific components of buyers' perceptions of food prices, taking care that the definitions employed are decision oriented and reasonably adequate for some subset of the population. The particular objectives established for this research are the measurement and explanation of perceptual validity at three levels.

1. Stores for which buyers' perceptions are most and least accurate.

2. Buyers whose perceptions are most and least accurate.

3. Groups of stores (neighborhoods) for which perceptions are most and least accurate.

Explanations for differences among and within these three levels will be investigated, including the perceptual process as well as the economic variables. Finally, the cost of specific misperceptions will be determined.

The potential contribution of perceptual economics can be assessed through this and similar studies. The findings of this study have action implications and economic significance for many participants. Only future research will tell whether this is an isolated or general instance, but the results are sufficiently encouraging to warrant further work in perceptual economics.

Chapter II

METHODOLOGY FOR MEASUREMENT OF BUYER PERCEPTUAL VALIDITY

The empirical side of this project was initially viewed as a study of pricing in the retail food industry and the perception of that pricing by various parties. We now see it as part of the larger subject of economic perception and misperception in general. The empirical work reported illustrates a general approach for studying the validity of perceptions, and the findings show the extent of misperception in a particular context.

The precise methods employed for studying buyers' perceptual validity will differ according to the purchase situation and the product involved. Several characteristics of food purchases are unique, but they all contribute to the conclusion that food purchasing is an interesting place to start the study of perceptual validity. Food is purchased frequently, and its purchase represents a familiar transaction. Large dollar amounts are at stake, even on a per transaction basis but particularly in terms of total annual expenditures. Thus, the study of perceptual validity in food purchases has the potential of great operational significance to the buyer. Substantial losses could be suffered if large differences exist among alternative offerings and are not perceived validly. Alternatively, large losses of time and effort could be incurred if the purchaser perceives differences among alternatives where none exists.

The measurement of perceptual validity requires three steps:

—A measure of the relevant reality.

—A measure of the comparable perception.

—A comparison of the two.

A procedure which is attractive to all researchers is to study what they know how to measure. If researchers insist that relevant realities should be studied, they are forced to consider the complexities of measuring real-world problems. Some sort of compromise is required in almost any research. A simple measure of that which is feasible but trivial must be resisted; at the same time, the important but unmanageably complex must be avoided. However, if research delves deeply enough, all problems possess elements of the latter. This is where simplifications— the stuff of which models are made—are introduced in order to make acceptable approximations.

Food purchase decisions are based upon many different factors: convenience, quality, cleanliness, price, services, and aesthetic appeal among others. All these factors are combined by the individual decision maker, with different weights assigned by each shopper. The problem is further complicated by the fact that the weights assigned may differ for different decisions and in different situations. Aesthetic appeal may be quite important when purchasing for a dinner party; convenience may be paramount for fill-in purchases; and nutrition may be overriding when buying for a new-born infant. Cleanliness may be considered essential in store selection, while price may be more important with respect to stock-up decisions.

The decision made by the food shopper should reflect her own value scale and her individual weights for the various factors. We do not view our task in this study as determining whether she made the right decision; rather we view our task as determining whether she perceived reality accurately. There is a big difference between these two! If she knows that a particular store is very high in price but chooses to shop there, we may disagree with her decision but should not accuse her of misperceiving. If she shops at a high priced store but does not know that it is high in price, that is another situation. If another shopper chooses a low service, dirty store because it offers very low prices, we may question the wisdom of that selection. But an appraisal of her perception would simply ask whether she is correct in stating that it is a low priced store.

The foregoing samples suggest that price perceptions might be a good starting point for the study of perceptual economics. We will classify the respondent as perceiving validly if she knows how much more or less she would pay for the various options open to her.

NEIGHBORHOODS STUDIED

Our field work was conducted in the summer of 1965 in five different cities designed to yield some environmental diversity. They were not intended to be representative of the nation. The five cities were

Greensboro, North Carolina; Havertown (a suburb of Philadelphia), Pennsylvania; New York City, New York; San Francisco, California; and St. Louis, Missouri.

Greensboro was selected because the Department of Agriculture had just completed a one-year study of food prices there, providing a possible base which could be extended. The remaining four cities met the twin criteria of geographic dispersion and the availability of supervisory personnel. Over 1000 personal interviews with consumers were conducted for the total study, and more than 60 different stores were included. Market basket indices based on approximately 80 different items were computed for each store in the study.

The neighborhood studied in each city was selected as an area in which shoppers had several equally convenient food stores as alternatives. The ideal area for our study was circular in shape with all of the major supermarkets in the area lying on the circumference of that circle. Smaller stores were permitted within the circumference, but no major supermarket could be so located. The consumers interviewed were at the "eye" of the circle; all the major supermarkets were equally accessible to them. This approach is the opposite of the typical retail study in which the stores are the center of the areas studied. The consumer is at the center for our study.

Each neighborhood included a variety of food store types: from very large to very small, some chains and some independents, from full service to limited service. Areas undergoing dramatic changes were excluded from consideration—changes such as the advent of a new store, the departure of an important store, the dropping of stamps by one of the stores, or the shift of an important store from "regular prices" to "discounting." Our objective was to study buyers' perceptions of price where reality might show large differences and where consumers had been able to observe such differences over a substantial length of time.

We tried to select five dissimilar neighborhoods—but not at the expense of the preceding criteria. We did not establish a formal structure for this dissimilarity, but we took into account such factors as socio-economic characteristics of the consumers and density of population. A complete census of all consumers at the eye was made in four of the cities, and a sampling fraction of one-half was employed in the fifth city (New York).[1]

---

[1] Summary statistics for selected socio-economic characteristics are reported for each of the five neighborhoods in Appendix A.

PRICE REALITY

The determination of price reality is not a simple task. The relevant measure depends upon the specific purchase decision, and the housewife has many decisions to make with respect to food purchasing. She must first decide what to buy. Her options ordinarily are numerous, and this choice is probably her most important decision. Price reality for this decision embraces the prices of alternative lists of items—each list constrained by family food desires.[2] When she has determined her list of items, then she must select the store at which she will make her purchase. A further decision, however, may be whether the purchases should be divided between two or more stores. Her composite decision designates the item(s) to be purchased, the store, the time, and the quantity. Some of her potential decisions are presented below. They are illustrative, but certainly not complete. Each refers to a different price reality.[3]

—Should I wait for specials? If yes, for which products? at which stores?

—Which stores should be excluded from my admissible set of stores?

—Should store evaluation be in terms of all food purchases or separately for sub-sets of food items? If for sub-sets, which sub-sets?

—Which sizes are the best "buys" for my family?

—Should I buy national brands or private brands? Should the decision be different for different products?

Our research project emphasizes comparisons among the price levels of competing stores in each neighborhood. The buyer's operational decision corresponding to this price dimension is store selection. The purchaser need not buy at the store with the lowest prices, but she should know how much additional she is paying for non-price factors. *Valid price perception does not imply that the shopper chooses the*

---

[2] Price comparisons for this decision would be particularly difficult because of the presence of non-price differences among the various lists.

[3] A comprehensive model of these different dimensions is presented in F. E. Brown, "Informational Requirements for Purchase Decisions," *Essays in Marketing Theory*, George Fisk (editor), Allyn and Bacon, Boston, Mass., 1971.

lowest price alternative but that she correctly perceives price differentials among alternatives.

What is the reality price for a food store? The price for each of 5000 to 8000 items helps to determine the true price reality. But how can all of these be combined into a single measure for a store's price level? The two main issues concern which items to sample and how to combine those sampled into a single figure.

Both of these problems are faced by the Bureau of Labor Statistics (BLS) in its Consumer Price Index, but a proper answer for the BLS may not be a proper answer for this investigation. The purposes of the two investigations are different. The BLS wishes to study price changes over time either for the entire country or for certain geographic areas. Our investigation focuses on comparisons at a point in time rather than across time.

This difference in purpose need not introduce a difference with respect to the appropriate items to include. The BLS survey of consumption patterns indicates the relative importance of each item, e.g., canned pears, eggs, bread, sugar.[4] This information is given on a city by city basis and shows the most important items for each city. The items with the highest weights are used in the Consumer Price Index and by the Department of Agriculture in its Greensboro study. The same logic applies to the present study. Those items with the highest weights for the nation comprise the list of items in our market basket.[5]

The selection of brands and sizes posed a problem not encountered by the BLS. The BLS does not compare price levels among stores; therefore, it does not need to price the same brand and size in all stores.[6] Since our comparisons are among stores, we need to price

[4]Detailed discussion of the methodology and findings of the BLS study are presented in "The Consumer Price Index," Bureau of Labor Statistics, Washington, D.C., 1962.

[5]Our market basket list of 76 products was the same in each city, but the weights used in calculating the indices were city specific. The weights used for Greensboro were determined for Durham. All others apply to precisely the same city. A limited number of products on the master list were not carried in some cities, but this number never exceeded four. The total number of items in the market basket exceeded 80 because some products were represented by more than one item, for example, both liquid and powdered detergent.

[6]The BLS does require that the same brand and size be held constant over time for a particular store even though it may differ among stores. In this way, comparisons over time reflect price changes, not changes in brands or sizes.

precisely the same items (including the same brands and sizes) in each of the stores to be compared. Otherwise the comparisons would reflect not only differences in price but differences in the composition of the market basket.

Pricing the same brand and size in each outlet raises other problems. It explicitly restricts the comparison of prices to those items that are the most popular and automatically eliminates private brands. It also excludes slow moving brands and sizes. Including private brands would introduce non-price factors into what should be a pure price comparison. Whether the physical products were the same or different would be immaterial; non-price elements would be introduced into the comparison. If we insist on identical brands and sizes, we run the risk that price relationships based upon them may not reflect price relationships for non-identical items.

We priced market baskets with identical brands and sizes in order to minimize non-price factors. A "consensus" brand and size, based upon inspection of the products on the shelves and conversations with those employed in the food establishments, was selected for each city. The resulting market basket was priced in each store on two different days within a seven day period. One observation was obtained early in the week (either Monday or Tuesday), and the second was obtained when week-end specials were in effect for the given community (ordinarily Friday but sometimes Thursday).

All pricing was performed by women trained by either the BLS for its Consumer Price Index or the Department of Agriculture for its one-year study in Greensboro. All prices were obtained by in-store shelf observations; in no case were they obtained from price lists or verbal statements from store employees. Each store manager was informed that the study was to be undertaken and that his store was to be a part ·of the study. He was not told the products or the brands to be covered in the study. The cooperation of the store manager was requested, and the pricers were instructed not to interfere with regular store business. Pricing took place even where cooperation was refused, typically being performed by the local project supervisor.

A subtle distinction exists between prices charged by a store and the amount a housewife may spend at a store. Market basket indices are designed to answer, "How much more or less would I pay for the same items?" They do not consider, "How much more or less will I end up spending if I shop there?" Stores carry different mixtures of private and national brands and offer different quality levels for the same product. They may also carry different product categories. Some stores have delicatessen departments; some have extensive non-food offerings; others have very limited offerings. A store may be low in price for standard items and charge exorbitant prices for items in which it has less competition. Market basket indices will not reflect differences in expenditures caused by the addition of items beyond the basic list or departures from it.

Should the more important items in the consumption pattern be weighted greater than those that are less important? From the point of view of the store, a weighted index will give a better measure of the overall pricing policies. Total sales volume is a weighted figure, and any attempt at profit analysis is based upon differential weights for different items. The cost to the consumer is also a weighted figure; she spends different amounts of money for different items. Indeed, the BLS survey weights reflect precisely this consumption pattern.

One might argue that the consumer evaluates price offerings of a store in a manner that is different from her consumption pattern. She may think of individual prices for 20 items as 20 observations each with the same significance, i.e., her perception may be formed in an "unweighted" manner. Such an argument would not change the price level of a store nor the total expenditures of a consumer. Therefore, price reality is measured in this investigation by a weighted market basket index using BLS items and weights.[7]

The market basket indices measure price reality adequately for the total neighborhood but not necessarily for each individual household. The market basket weights were determined for each city and reflect the consumption pattern for the aggregate of all consumers. Although these weights were not determined for the specific neighborhood, they should be a good approximation of reality for any large group of consumers. The market basket may be inappropriate, however, for individual households who have consumption patterns that differ greatly from the community norm. Perhaps we should have adjusted for these differences, but we considered it too difficult a task—at least at this stage in the development of perceptual economics. This possible discrepancy means that some individuals may be misclassified with respect to perceptual validity. It also means that total neighborhood classification should be on a firm base.

[7]Details concerning the index number calculation are presented in Appendix D.

MEASUREMENT OF PRICE PERCEPTION

Price perception as supplied by the respondent ideally should correspond to the market basket index as calculated. We did not consider it feasible to explain the mathematical calculation of the market basket index to the respondent and ask her to make an estimate of the resulting figures for each of the stores. Not having done that, how can we compare a perception supplied by the respondent with a price reality concept that was unknown to her?

If all consumers purchase the same products in the same quantities and the market basket index is based on that consumption pattern, no problem exists. Each respondent can be asked to compare the price levels of the stores. Since customers do not all buy the same products, we moved a little beyond the simple price level question. Consumers were asked to rate the stores with respect to price levels "for goods of equal quality." Respondents occasionally stated that the stores did not have the same general quality levels. Interviewers were instructed in that case to ask for comparisons based on items which were of the same quality. In retrospect, we possibly should have told the respondent more about the nature of the market basket index.

Respondents found it almost impossible to rate stores with respect to price levels on either a ratio or interval scale. The questionnaire was lengthy and rapport was hindered by attempting to push the respondent on this question. If fewer topics had been covered in the interview, perhaps interval scale ratings could have been obtained. Respondents even had difficulty with complete ordinal rankings where six or more stores were being compared. The questionnaire went through 15 separate drafts, eight of which were field tested. Most of the difficulty centered around the question of securing price perceptions on as precise a scale as possible. We finally settled for an incomplete ordinal scale in which the respondent was asked to identify the lowest, second lowest, highest, and second highest stores in price.[8]

The possibility of probing for price perceptions raises certain dangers. Does such probing reveal unconscious perceptions the housewife has already formed, or does it force the housewife to manufacture perceptions—perceptions that were not formed prior to the interview? However gross it may be, the housewife's perception should be appraised for validity at the level of precision she employs. If ordinal

[8]For the specific wording of the questions, see the questionnaire in Appendix B.

rankings are perceived by the housewife, perceptual validity should be measured at that level. But very gross perceptions raise measurement problems. What is the meaning of "a little bit lower in price?" Does it have a monetary connotation? How about "much higher?" The basic research problem here is how to obtain from the respondent conscious or hidden perceptions on as precise a scale as possible. We want the respondent to reveal her perceptions in sufficient detail, but we must not force her to manufacture numbers in order to placate the interviewer.

The approach used for our research probed to a very limited extent—trying to secure from each respondent the incomplete ordinal scale. We then sought to uncover somewhat greater precision, applying various analytic devices but using only ideas that were implicit in the responses obtained.

One approach to the measurement of perceptual validity required an overall price perception scale for each neighborhood. This result was achieved on an interval scale in two steps. First, the incomplete ordinal scale supplied by each respondent was converted into a series of paired comparisons. Second, the aggregate results of the paired comparisons were transformed into an interval scale using Thurstone's law of comparative judgments.

The procedure assumes that each respondent implicitly made a series of paired comparisons by stating her ordinal scale. For example, when a respondent ranked store B next to the lowest in price, she implicitly compared store B with store A, store C, etc. and placed it lower than all except one.

TABLE 1
PERCEIVED PRICE LEVELS CALCULATED
FROM PAIRED COMPARISONS

Second Store	First Store[a]					Perceived Price Level
	A	B	C	D	E	
A		35	10	20	14	-1.01
B	65		22	33	25	-0.41
C	90	78		61	56	+0.69
D	80	67	39		45	+0.24
E	86	75	44	55		+0.48

[a]Percentage rating second store higher than first.

Table 1 presents illustrative data for an entire neighborhood. It shows that store C was usually rated higher in price than the other four stores: 90 percent of the respondents stated that C had higher prices than A; 78 percent, that it had higher prices than B; etc. Store A, however, was almost always rated lower in price. Perceived price levels were computed from these paired comparisons (see the last column of Table 1).[9] The results show that store A is one standard deviation below the mean and C is approximately 2/3 standard deviation above the mean. The resulting interval scale for perception is expressed in standard scores and not in monetary units. The interval between stores cannot be converted into a dollar figure or a percentage figure without additional assumptions.[10]

Several other dimensions of consumer price perceptions were also recorded: departmental price levels, overall range of prices among competing stores, and price variations for individual items. Naming of the highest priced store and the lowest priced store for each department provided departmental price perceptions. We measured perceived overall price variability among stores by a simple question asking for the perceived difference between the highest and lowest priced stores. Perceived price variations for individual items was measured on two bases: perceived differences at the same store over a three week interval and the perceived range among competing stores on the same day.

MEASUREMENT OF PERCEPTUAL VALIDITY

The principal dimension of perceptual validity in our study is store selection for the aggregate market basket index. We measured perceptual validity for this dimension in two respects: the aggregate for all consumers within a neighborhood and individually for each respondent within that neighborhood.

Two different approaches to the measurement of neighborhood perceptual validity are possible: (1) comparison between price reality

[9]For a discussion of the rationale and calculation of Thurstone's law of comparative judgments see L. L. Thurstone, *The Measurement of Values,* Chicago, Ill.: The University of Chicago Press, 1959.

[10]Technically, the scales are interval but not ratio. The market basket indices, however, are ratio scales.

and a consensus price perception for all respondents and (2) an average of individual validity measures, determined separately for each respondent.

The first approach might classify the neighborhood perception as valid despite the presence of large individual misperceptions—if those misperceptions offset each other. Thus, this approach might be a test for offsetting errors rather than for perceptual validity. If there is close agreement between reality and perception by this approach, the validity of individual perceptions will have to be checked. Lack of close agreement will indicate invalid perceptions and non-offsetting errors. The second approach—averaging individual validity scores—is preferable, but the incomplete ordinal scores of this project are analytically less powerful when we use them on an individual basis. Both approaches will be presented, but we place more stress on the consensus approach.

We can judge perceptual validity for the entire neighborhood by comparing the interval scales for reality and perception.[11] If the scores for price reality and price perception are identical, perception is perfect; if the scores are approximately the same, perception is reasonably good. A comparison between the two sets of scores for hypothetical data is shown in Figure 1. The solid diagonal through the origin indicates the positions in which the scores for perception and reality are identical. The broken lines, parallel to it, correspond to differences of one standard deviation between the two scores. (The two scales have been transformed into standard scores in order to show deviations from the mean as the number of standard deviations.) Four of the five stores (all except B) received approximately the same score for both perceived price and actual price—shown by the fact that all four are between the two broken lines and close to the main diagonal.

---

[11] This discussion uses the first approach suggested and ignores the possibility of offsetting misperceptions. That possibility will be investigated when empirical results are presented. The danger that offsetting errors will yield aggregate perceptual scores that agree with price reality is less when using paired comparisons than would be the case with data collected initially on an interval scale. Misperceptions in opposite directions would result in paired comparisons that were closer to a 50-50 split than reality would warrant. This in turn would cause a lack of agreement between reality and the aggregate price perception score. The same misperceptions could yield valid aggregate perceptions if the individual data were collected on an interval scale.

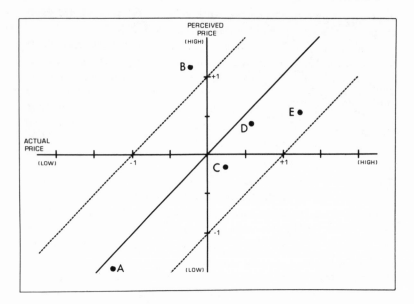

Figure 1. Price Perception vs. Price Reality, Hypothetical Data.

Store B was perceived as the highest priced store although it was next to the lowest in market basket index.

There are no absolute standards for valid or invalid perceptions, but higher r^2 values mean more valid perceptions while lower r^2 values mean less valid perceptions. The r^2 value associated with the data in Figure 1 is almost .50.

Standards for judging whether specific stores are validly or invalidly perceived are likewise arbitrary. The standards within this project are those designated by the broken lines on Figure 1. Any store for which perception is within one standard deviation of its market basket price will be considered "validly perceived," and any store for which the difference is more than one standard deviation will be considered "misperceived."

The principal weaknesses of this aggregate measure of perceptual validity stem from properties of the market basket and the price perception scale already discussed. The market basket is based on over 80 items and refers to a specific point in time. Either of these factors could make the indices faulty measures of reality; but we believe them reasonably representative. Prior work by the food commission and some of our own supplementary work indicate that indices based upon samples of this size yield rather stable results over time.[12]

We measured the perceptual validity for individual respondents by comparing each respondent's ordinal rankings with the market basket rankings. Perfect perception is indicated by a zero—no disagreement between the two rankings. The higher the score, the greater the disagreement. This scale assigns a larger penalty for a shift in rankings between stores that have large differences in price indices than for a shift of stores that have small differences.

TABLE 2
CALCULATION OF INDIVIDUAL
PERCEPTUAL VALIDITY SCORES

| Store | *Market Basket Price Index* | *Respondents' Rankings* | | |
		I	*II*	*III*
A	.975	1	2	1
B	.990	2	1	4
C	1.015	3	3	3
D	1.020	4	4	2

Scoring for Individual Respondents:

I No errors	Score	.0000
II Incorrect Paired Comparisons:	AB	.015
	Score	.0025
III Incorrect Paired Comparisons:	BC	.025
	BD	.030
	CD	.005
		.060
	Score	.0100

Table 2 illustrates the calculation of perceptual validity scores for three respondents in a city with four stores. Respondent I was assigned a perfect score of 0 because her ranking corresponded perfectly with the ranking of the market basket indices. Respondent II was incorrect for only one of six paired comparisons; she switched the positions for A and B. Her score is the mean error per paired

[12]See *Organization and Competition in Food Retailing,* Technical Study No. 7, National Commission on Food Marketing, Washington, D.C., June 1966; and F. E. Brown, "Supermarket Pricing," *The Southern Journal of Business,* April 1969, p. 317.

comparison (.015 ÷ 6 = .0025). Respondent III was incorrect for three paired comparisons; Table 2 shows the calculation of her score.[13]

The measurement of individual perceptual validity has the limitation already indicated, viz., the market basket index may not be the appropriate measure of price reality for a particular respondent even if it is satisfactory for the community as a whole. The validity measure also assumes that it is equally important for the respondent to place a store correctly at each rank, i.e., decision making will not be affected differently by an improper classification of a low priced store than by improper classification of a high or middle priced store. The rationale for this position is that the shopper does not base her decision solely on price. The validity of her price perception is determined by whether she can judge how much more or less she will pay by shopping at the various stores. Correct identification of the low priced store by one shopper may have less significance for her decisions than correct identification of the high priced store. For another shopper, the reverse may be true. Without a sound basis for weighting the importance of specific comparisons for individual consumers, we have weighted each equally.

The second approach to determining the validity of neighborhood perceptions uses average individual perceptual validity. This raw arithmetic mean reflects both the magnitude of price differences among the stores of the neighborhood and consumer ability to discriminate. If all stores within a neighborhood have approximately the same price levels, the average error will be small even if perceptions are inaccurate. A better indicator of perceptual validity compares the average individual validity score to a random result. Table 3 shows hypothetical figures for two communities.

The average error in community A is much lower than that in B, but the average error in A would be small even if the rankings were chosen at random. A comparison between the neighborhood average and the random result shows an improvement over chance of 33% in community A but over 60% in community B (last column). This mean validity score is a more accurate indicator of neighborhood discriminatory power.[14]

---

[13]Appendix F illustrates the calculation of perceptual validity in more complicated situations.

[14]It should be recognized that the shoppers in B may be facing an easier task than those in A, but the payoff for valid perceptions is also greater in B than in A.

TABLE 3
CALCULATION OF MEAN PERCEPTUAL VALIDITY

Community	Mean Error (Unadjusted)	Random Result	Mean Validity
A	.010	.015	.333
B	.030	.080	.625

Measures of perceptual validity for other dimensions and decisions are much less involved and less precise. But the task is basically the same for each: a comparison of price reality and price perception—measured in ways as similar as possible. But even more important, the price reality should conform to an operationally significant purchase decision.

We measure the validity of price perceptions for the range among stores by a simple comparison between perceived price range and the range for market basket indices. The validity of departmental perceptions is evaluated with two general approaches. (1) The stores with the highest and lowest market basket indices for each department (for example, fresh meat) are compared to the consensus rankings for high and low priced stores for that department. (2) Consistency of a store's price levels across departments is compared to the consistency perceived by consumers across departments. The validity of perceptions with regard to price variations in individual items is shown by a direct comparison between observed and perceived price range among stores on the same day and within a store over a three week period.

EXPLANATIONS OF PERCEPTUAL VALIDITY

The empirical portion of this study is more concerned with the description of perceptual validity than with its explanation. This is the result of necessity rather than interest. Our first task was to establish a method of measuring perceptual validity and to demonstrate that this method could be applied to real-life situations. Our next task was to explain the magnitude of misperception and the differentials in perceptual validity; our project has only produced fragmentary and exploratory results on this second task.

Since there are three levels for describing perceptual validity (neighborhood, specific store, and individual consumer), there are also three levels for explaining perceptual validity. At the community level, our project has a sample size of only five and a non-random sample at that. Any explanations of community differences in perceptual validity must be conjectural; the kinds of variables considered refer to the environment of competitive stores and the shopping and socio-economic characteristics of shoppers within that environment. Logical environmental variables considered refer to the similarity of store characteristics such as services offered, size of stores, and variability in market basket indices. Explanatory variables for misperceptions of individual stores seem to be these same variables, particularly those which distinguish a store from others in the neighborhood. Sample size is also small for individual stores, roughly 60 although only 27 are supermarkets. Explanatory variables tested at the individual shopper level are in three categories: shopping attitudes, shopping behavior, and socio-economic characteristics. The empirical work in this area focuses on differences among shoppers within the same neighborhood.

Analytic techniques for studying explanatory variables at the neighborhood and store levels were extremely simple—not extending beyond rank correlation. The analysis at the individual consumer level uses step-wise multiple regression.[15] The computer program specified that no independent variable was to be added to the equation unless the F ratio was significant at the .05 level. The five resulting equations (one for each neighborhood) provide the base for determining which variables are most closely related to individual perceptual validity. We calculated a second multiple regression equation using all of the independent variables studied—again one equation for each community. This set of equations permits a test across cities for the consistency of the direction of relationship between each variable and individual perceptual validity.

SUMMARY

The empirical work for this study took place in the summer of 1965 in five different communities, representing five case studies but using the same methodology. We measured price reality and price perception for

[15]Factor analysis revealed that several potential explanatory variables were inter-related. Any variables with heavy loadings on the same factor were merged into one independent variable. Some variables were dichotomous or trichotomous and were handled as dummy variables. The specific variables and the transformations are indicated in Appendix G.

several food purchase decisions, with principal emphasis on overall store selection. We accept the comparisons between the two measures as our best estimates of the validity of price perceptions. Weaknesses and limitations of the methods are acknowledged, but the results represent what we believe to be the first empirical attempt to measure perceptual validity in a non-laboratory business setting. Perceptual validity is measured at three levels: the validity with which a total neighborhood of competing food stores is perceived, the validity with which individual food stores are perceived, and the validity of perceptions formed by individual food shoppers. Together, they illustrate methods for studying perceptual validity and the results that can be obtained from such studies.

The Accuracy
of Housewives'
Price Perceptions:
Empirical Findings

Price perceptions for food items differ from price reality. Misperceptions abound but are not uniformly distributed among housewives, communities, or all decisions. The empirical results of this study can be conveniently grouped into three categories: (1) for complete neighborhoods, (2) for specific stores, and (3) for individual shoppers. Wide differences exist within each of these categories. We examine the magnitude of these differences and potential explanations in Chapters III-V, each directed to one of the three levels of analysis. Part II concludes with an investigation of the economic significance of price misperceptions for food items (Chapter VI).

Chapter III

NEIGHBORHOOD PERCEPTUAL ACCURACY: SOME GOOD, SOME BAD

Large differences exist in the accuracy of price perceptions formed in different neighborhoods. In two of the areas studied, perceptions were remarkably good—Greensboro and Havertown. In two others, the perceptions were grossly in error—St. Louis and San Francisco. The fifth city (New York) occupied an intermediate position.

The array of competing food stores facing shoppers varies considerably among neighborhoods. Each neighborhood has its own mix of stores, differing not only in price offerings but also in non-price characteristics. In some neighborhoods, price levels may be highly similar; while in others, there may be wide variations. With a wide diversity of store environments, a wide diversity in the accuracy of consumers' perceptions from neighborhood to neighborhood is not surprising.

Shoppers in all five cities agreed on the general cues that are associated with high or low prices. These cues fit into two general relationships: stores that incur additional costs will charge higher prices, and stores that generate a high volume of activity will have low prices. These two tendencies sometimes operate in the same direction and sometimes offset each other. Neighborhoods in which these cues were consistent with price levels were neighborhoods in which price perceptions were more accurate. Neighborhoods in which these cues were not consistent with market basket indices were neighborhoods in which price perceptions were less accurate.

The empirical results also permit conclusions that go beyond food purchases. Inaccurate perceptions do exist; reality and perception do not necessarily coincide. The loss from inaccurate perception and decisions resulting from misperceptions may be of substantial magnitude. In food shopping the difference in price among supermarkets is typically 5-10% while the difference if both supermarkets and small stores are included is often 20-25%. The results also indicate that substantive conclusions for one neighborhood may be quite inaccurate in another; we must investigate each neighborhood and each decision separately. Finally the results indicate that empirical research in the field of perceptual economics is feasible. The measuring instruments employed in this project need improvement, but their current precision is sufficient to show that neighborhoods differ in perceptual accuracy.

Perceptual accuracy is pertinent for every buying decision. Only a few decisions are investigated in this project, but the general approach could be modified for other decisions. Store selection, whether for a total food order or a portion of a food order, is a decision made by every shopper. This is the principal decision considered in this project. To store owners, this is obviously a crucial shopper decision. To manufacturers and wholesalers, this decision has great significance for distribution policies. Public policy agents share the consumer's concern, and the price reality data of the study will show the economic significance of the decision for the consumer. Other decisions investigated in less detail are the timing of purchases and the wisdom of buying sub-groups of products at different stores rather than buying the entire market basket at a single store.

SMALL STORE PRICES VERSUS SUPERMARKET PRICES

Most consumers draw sharp distinctions between small food stores and supermarkets. The typical respondent in our preliminary investigations did not believe the small store could satisfy her major food shopping needs. She also indicated that she perceived price levels of supermarkets and small food stores as quite different. Most of our analyses will be restricted to the supermarkets, but first we will examine the accuracy of price perceptions for small stores in contrast to supermarkets.

The generalization that small food stores have higher price levels than supermarkets is valid. On the average the small stores were about 8% higher in price, and 28 of 36 small stores had higher price levels than any neighborhood supermarket (see Table 1). As long as the reality for a particular environment conforms to this generalization, consumers have valid perceptions concerning supermarket versus small store price relationships. When such a general theory does not apply, misperceptions are likely to occur.

In New York the price level for small stores was within ¼% of the supermarket average. New York consumers failed to ·perceive this near

TABLE 1
SMALL STORE PRICE LEVELS VS.
SUPERMARKET PRICE LEVELS

Community	*Small Store Figures*		
	Mean Price Index[a]	*No. Above Supermarket Mean*[b]	*No. Above All Supermarkets*[b]
Greensboro	1.09	7 (8)	7 (8)
Havertown	1.19	6 (6)	6 (6)
New York	1.00	4 (6)	3 (6)
St. Louis	1.09	9 (9)	8 (9)
San Francisco	1.03	6 (7)	4 (7)
TOTAL	1.08	32 (36)	28 (36)

[a]Supermarket price average equals 1.00.

[b]The number of small food stores studied is shown in parentheses.

equality, attributing substantially higher prices to the small stores. Consumers consistently said that the small stores were higher in price than any of the supermarkets (79% as shown by Table 2). Market basket indices showed two of the six small stores as below average in price level and a third well within the supermarket range. One New York small store was actually lower in price than any of the supermarkets, a fact correctly perceived by only one respondent in the entire sample.

The differential between small stores and supermarkets was 3% in San Francisco, but shoppers there were more likely to recognize the low prices of specific small stores than were New York shoppers. Almost half of the consumers ranked these specific small stores within the supermarket price range. These results do not give the low priced small stores as much credit as they deserve, but the San Francisco shoppers showed less misperception than their New York counterparts.

Perceptions concerning the price relationships between supermarkets and small stores were generally more accurate in the other three communities. Reality was much more in line with the intuitive generalization in these communities, showing differences of 9-19%. Only one of the 23 small stores in these communities had lower than average prices.

TABLE 2
PERCEPTIONS OF SMALL STORE PRICES

Community	Percentage Ranking Specific Small Store Higher Than Any Supermarket[a]	Percentage Ranking General Small Stores As "High" in Price[b]
Greensboro[c]	80	95
Havertown	91	86
New York	79	81
St. Louis	90	93
San Francisco	51	86
TOTAL	78	88

[a]Rankings in column 2 refer to specific small stores of the community. Respondents rated only the small stores with which they were familiar.

[b]Percentage of consumers who said "a small store" was likely to have "high" prices, as opposed to "low" or "average." See questionnaire in Appendix B.

[c] Greensboro questionnaire employed a slightly different wording. The respondent was asked to classify each store as "much higher than others," "higher than others," "about the middle," "lower than others," or "much lower than others." The percentage in column 2 included ratings of either much higher or higher.

Consumers were asked the general price level for 11 different kinds of stores. Each one was described by a short phrase, for example, a new store, a store that offers a wide assortment, or a store that advertises a lot. One of these descriptors was "a small store." The small store was rated as "high" in price more often than any of the other 11 types of stores, over 80% of the consumers in each city (see Table 2). It is consequently very difficult for a small store to receive a low price image from consumers even when such an image is justified.

This deductive process of applying a broad generalization to specific stiuations occurred in several phases of our research. It is one of the more pervasive results. Misperceptions often occur when the environmental situation is contrary to intuitive or logical generalizations. The generalization, not the facts, gives rise to the perception. The facts seldom alter a logical conclusion.

NEIGHBORHOOD SUPERMARKET PRICE PERCEPTIONS

We shift now to the consideration of only supermarkets. The validity of neighborhood perception of supermarket prices ranged from excellent to zero. r^2 values between aggregate price perception and market basket indices are shown in Table 3. They indicate that a single measure for perceptual validity for all areas is inappropriate; each neighborhood calls for a separate appraisal.

TABLE 3
NEIGHBORHOOD PERCEPTUAL ACCURACY:
A COMPARISON OF TWO MEASURES

Community	r^2	Mean Individual Accuracy
Greensboro	.90	.75
Havertown	.81	.68
New York	.06	.21
St. Louis	.00	.00
San Francisco	.00	.01

Note: r^2 values are adjusted for degrees of freedom. Methodology for the two measures is detailed in Chapter II, pages 28-33.

Greensboro and Havertown shoppers show excellent perceptions, with r^2's of .90 and .81. New Yorkers' perceptions reveal limited accuracy, but the results for St. Louis and San Francisco indicate almost zero validity for their shoppers.

The aggregate perception by Havertown and Greensboro shoppers was correct for both the store with the highest price level and the one with the lowest price level. No store in either neighborhood was misperceived by as much as one standard deviation.[1] The low priced store was correctly perceived in New York, but the high priced store was not properly placed. Only one store in this community was misperceived by more than one standard deviation. St. Louis and San

---

[1] In both Havertown and Greensboro two of the supermarkets studied belonged to the same chain. The analysis presented here treats these two stores separately in contrast to the results presented in F. E. Brown, "Price Image Versus Price Reality," *Journal of Marketing Research*, May 1969.

Francisco shoppers failed to identify either the high priced store or the low priced store, and about half of the stores in each city were misperceived by more than one standard deviation. Figures 1 and 2 illustrate these relationships, using as examples the Havertown and San Francisco data.

Mean perceptual accuracy for shoppers in St. Louis and San Francisco was no better than would be expected from chance selection of stores (see column 3 of Table 3). Marked perceptual ability was recorded by Greensboro and Havertown shoppers—mean scores in these communities showing improvement of 2/3 to 3/4 over chance. New York shoppers were 20% better than random selection. The results, as shown in Table 3, are remarkably similar with the two approaches.

Are Misperceptions Offsetting?

The results for New York, San Francisco, and St. Louis show extensive misperceptions and the failure of these misperceptions to offset each other. In each case the misperceptions reinforce each other. Store B in San Francisco, for example, had the second lowest prices among seven competing supermarkets but was perceived as next to the highest in

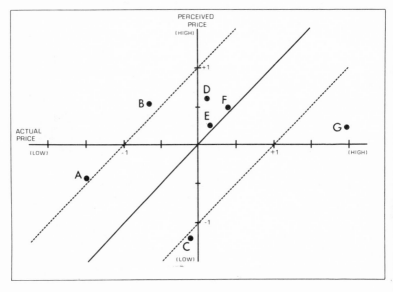

Figure 1. Price Perception vs. Price Reality, San Francisco.

price (see Figure 1). Forty-five percent of the housewives placed it either highest or second highest, in contrast to 4% who placed it lowest or second lowest.

The high r^2 values for Greensboro and Havertown were produced by accurate individual perceptions, not by offsetting misperceptions. The mean individual accuracy scores demonstrate this general ability as does the large number of shoppers who identified the highest and lowest priced stores—almost 75% in each instance.

EXPLANATIONS OF NEIGHBORHOOD PERCEPTUAL ACCURACY

It should be easier for shoppers to discriminate among stores when those stores differ appreciably in price levels. Shoppers also have greater incentive and payoff for accurate discrimination in such cases. The two neighborhoods for which price levels among competing supermarkets were most similar were San Francisco and St. Louis. The total range of price indices in San Francisco was only 2½% and that in St. Louis only 3½% (see Table 4). These were the two neighborhoods in which price perceptions were least accurate. The total range from lowest to highest

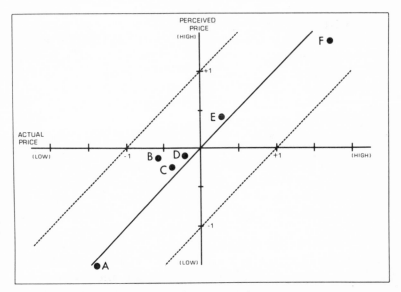

Figure 2. Price Perception vs. Price Reality, Havertown.

stores in both New York and Greensboro was over 7½%. The result was that perception was more accurate in these two cities. The evidence for Havertown is less consistent with this hypothesis, having a price range of only 3.9%. The relationship between neighborhood perceptual accuracy and price range for the five cities is shown by the positive rank correlation of .48.

TABLE 4
ACCURACY OF PRICE PERCEPTIONS VS. PRICE RANGE

| Community | Perceptual Accuracy Rank | Price Range | | No. of Stores |
		Percent	Rank	
Greensboro	1	7.5	2	6[a]
Havertown	2	3.9	3	6[a]
New York	3	7.7	1	4
St. Louis	4.5	3.6	4	6
San Francisco	4.5	2.4	5	7

ρ (adjusted for degrees of freedom) = .48

[a]Six supermarkets were studied in both Greensboro and Havertown, but two stores in each community were from the same chain.

A consumer should be able to discriminate among the price levels of three or four stores more easily than among the price levels of eight or ten stores. Our project was not well designed to test this hypothesis, but the evidence gives some support to it. For example, San Francisco consumers were asked to appraise the largest number of different stores (seven), and their perceptual accuracy was quite low. The remaining evidence is not strong but still consistent with the hypothesis, particularly if we consider the number of different chains rather than the number of different stores. In both Greensboro and Havertown, two stores of the same chain were studied. Thus in the two communities which recorded the most accurate perceptions, there were only five different chains.

That housewives perceive supermarket prices inaccurately is not at all surprising when we recognize the degree of confusion present in the real world of food prices. If a store with a market basket index of .98 were consistently 2% below the neighborhood average for all products, consumers could easily form accurate perceptions of that store's price level. But low priced stores are not low on all items, and high priced stores are not high on all items.

An indication of the confusion is seen by a crude test for price consistency. How many items are priced above average in a store that has a below average price index? Or conversely, how many items are priced below average in a store that has an above average price index? The median answer to each question is approximately 35%! Only one store in the entire study fell below 20%. The store with the fewest items above average was the lowest priced store in St. Louis, and even it had 19.5% of its market basket items above the neighborhood average. The store with the fewest items below average was a medium priced store (also in St. Louis) that was below average for only 21.9% of the items in the market basket. Every single store in our sample had the lowest prices for some items and the highest prices for other items. This "scrambled" pricing reality poses an extremely complex information-processing task for the consumer.

Is there a short cut to the formation of accurate perceptions by the consumer? Can she settle for a small list of products which represent the general price level? The store tries to guess the items that consumers may use for such a list and stresses its low prices on those items. Bob Holdren has identified products with a high "transfer effect"—calling them "k" type products. He states that consumers will switch store patronage for price reductions on certain kinds of products.[2] Whether such products exist is not the question at the moment; what does matter is that retailers' pricing policies can distort the appropriateness of any small list of items as reliable indicators of a store's average price level.

The Use and Misuse of Cues

Faced with the inappropriateness of a small list of items and the complexity of processing a large market basket index, many housewives seem to rely on operating characteristics of the stores rather than on an analysis of actual prices. If this is true, accurate perceptions should result where cues are appropriate. If cues are not universally applicable, their use in forming perceptions may lead to error—at least in some instances. The general price levels that housewives associate with stores of different types are presented in Table 5 (store types with low numbers are those for which the perceived price level is most likely to be low). The remarkable similarity that exists among communities in

[2]Bob R. Holdren, *The Structure of Retail Markets and the Market Behavior of Retail Units,* Prentice-Hall, Inc., p. 140.

TABLE 5
PERCEIVED PRICE LEVEL FOR VARIOUS TYPES OF STORES[a]

Type	Havertown	Greensboro	New York	San Francisco	St. Louis
New	2	1	1	1	1
Untidy	1	2	3	5[b]	2
Large shopping center	4	5[b]	2	2	3
Lots of advertising	3	3	5	4	4
Wide assortment	5	4	4	3[b]	5
Loss leaders	6	6	7	7	7
Trading stamps	7	10[b]	6	6	6
Expensive interior	9	7.5	8	8.5	9
Open late	8	7.5	9	10	8
Extra services	10	9	10	8.5	10
Small	11	11	11	11	11

[a]Perceived price levels are ranked from low to high: "1" for lowest to "11" for highest.

[b]Differs from overall rating by more than one rank.

the types of stores consumers expect to have high and low prices is shown by the high coefficient of concordance (.92).[3]

The near-unanimity with which consumers classify price levels of different types of stores can be fitted into a general pattern. As a first dimension, consumers believe that extra costs incurred by a store will be reflected in higher prices. Extra services, late hours, expensive interiors, and trading stamps—in that order—are viewed as signs of high prices. As a second dimension, large volume operations create an impression of lower prices. A large shopping center, lots of advertising, and a wide assortment—all associated with volume operations—are accepted as cues for lower prices. At the other extreme, a small store is considered the strongest indicator of high prices, ranking at the top in every community.

The hypothesis that consumers use higher expenses for the store as a cue for higher prices was tested in each of the five neighborhoods. Assuming that housewives used number of services and quality of fresh meats and produce as indicators of higher expenses, we tested for

[3]The limits of the coefficient of concordance are 0.0 and 1.0. See Merle W. Tate and Richard C. Clelland, *Nonparametric and Shortcut Statistics,* Interstate Printers and Publishers Inc., Danville, Ill., p. 19.

TABLE 6
PERCEIVED QUALITY AND NUMBER OF
SERVICES AS EXPLANATORY VARIABLES
FOR PERCEIVED PRICE[a]

Community	Perceived Quality Versus Perceived Price	Number of Services Versus Perceived Price
Greensboro	.86	.00
Havertown	.00	.57
New York	.20	N.A.[b]
San Francisco	.00	.83
St. Louis	.44	.00

[a]Coefficients of rank correlation; ρ adjusted for degrees of freedom.

[b]N. A. = Not available.

relationships between higher expenses and perceived price level in contrast to relationships between higher expenses and market basket indices.[4] Either quality level or number of services was in fact correlated with perceived price in each of the neighborhoods (see Table 6). These results (using a coefficient of rank correlation) contrast sharply with the lack of association found between the market basket indices and these two indicators of extra expenses.[5]

These findings sketch the beginnings of a model which links operating characteristics of stores to perception via cues involving expenses and volume. Interesting questions arise regarding relative weights that housewives give to various input factors—including different aspects of reality, how these weights are determined, and whether the weights change over time. These points will be considered in more detail in Chapter VI. We have established at this point that

[4]Difficult measurement problems were encountered in trying to test this hypothesis. Number of services offered and perceived quality of fresh meats and produce are very crude measures of extra expenses. The first was determined by personal count by the local project supervisor; the second, by the consumer interview. Further details are given in Appendix E.

[5]The coefficients of rank correlation were equal to zero when market basket index as distinct from perceived price was employed. It was impossible to distinguish between perceived price and market basket index for Havertown and Greensboro where there was perfect rank correlation between the two. The analysis combined stores of the same chain since consumers considered them identical in price level.

communities differ significantly in the accuracy of their perceptions, and we have identified some promising explanatory variables for this phenomenon.

Misperceptions Unlikely To Be Offsetting

The finding that misperceptions are not offsetting is perfectly consistent with armchair speculation. We would expect the principal sources of misperception to create a net imbalance. These sources can be grouped into four broad categories:

(1) The conscious efforts of sellers to create favorable impressions of their offerings.

(2) The unconscious efforts of buyers to believe things that satisfy their own personality needs.

(3) Perceptual failures due to such factors as ignorance, haste, lack of interest or information.

(4) The effect of consumer-leaders who pass on to others their own misperceptions.

The fourth may be considered a repetition of the first three points as they uniquely affect a particular group of individuals.

Every vendor is expected to put the best interpretation he can on all of his actions and to create the most favorable impression he can for his products, prices, and services. That is "just plain good business." One cannot find many businessmen who do not act this way or who consider such behavior offensive. Moreover, almost every customer knows that businessmen try to create favorable impressions, rather than to convey an accurate impression of their offerings. The awareness of vendors' motives, the existence of legal restrictions, and the limits of customer gullibility all combine to protect consumers against gross misperceptions. Nevertheless, we must not underrate the ingenuity and skill of sellers.

The consumer's problem is complicated further by the uneven distribution of promotional skills. Sellers differ substantially in their ability to create favorable impressions of their offerings. Rather than offsetting errors, we might expect the skilled promoter to create a systematic bias in his own favor. Conversely, the unskilled seller—on a relative basis—must be viewed less favorably by customers than reality justifies.

It is possible that buyers want to believe certain things that are not so about product offerings. Their deep desire to gain in physical attractiveness, health, self-realization, personal enjoyment, prestige, admiration—all of the things that vendors claim to offer—may unconsciously lead them to believe the incredible. This type of misperception differs from the first because the buyer, rather than the seller, creates or adds to the error. Misperceptions to which the buyer contributes are not likely to be offsetting. We would expect a strong bias in the direction of products with highly emotional overtones. If this kind of bias exists, misperceptions based on rationalization would disturb the industrial composition of the economy even more than they would disturb the within-industry structure.

The capacity and desire to perceive accurately probably differ among individuals. To perceive and interpret market phenomena requires intelligence, information, and sophistication concerning sellers' business practices, the effects of competition, and government regulation. Very often in the search for information, accurate perceptions require effort and expense. Market search may involve a delay in making a purchase that the buyer is strongly impelled to make then and there. An unwillingness to make a large effort or to incur an expense to get information might explain the misperceptions of many buyers.

The effect of consumer-leaders on the market mechanism depends on the accuracy of their perceptions. At the first stage, they are subject to the same three forces (for misperception) as consumers who imitate their buying practices. At the second stage, the effects of their misperceptions are multiplied. If in the aggregate the perceptions of consumer-leaders are more accurate than those of other buyers, their influence on the market structure should be beneficial; if not, their influence would be disturbing. It does appear—but we do not know for sure—that the influentials of a community are a fairly distinct social group and exhibit behavior configurations that are similar to each other. If we accept this pattern, the consumer-leaders are a significant force working toward a consensus. Hence, the relative accuracy of their perceptions is a matter worthy of investigation.

The first two sources of misperception (sellers' efforts and buyers' unconscious desires) are not likely to produce offsetting results. Their net effect would tend to create distortions in the market mechanism rather than offsetting errors. The effect of the other two sources on market allocations and market share is less obvious. Our empirical results with respect to individual shoppers (Chapter V) does not yield an altogether consistent picture.

PERCEPTUAL ACCURACY: OTHER DIMENSIONS

The accuracy of price perceptions varies with different decisions. We have seen that neighborhoods differ significantly in their ability to perceive the price levels of competing stores. Do the neighborhoods with the most accurate perceptions on that dimension also perceive more accurately on other dimensions? Are there dimensions which all five neighborhoods perceive with high or low accuracy? These and related questions will be investigated in this section as we expand our coverage to several additional dimensions of food prices.

Departmental Price Levels

Consumer perceptions of departmental price levels are generally poor. The typical consumer views a store as charging the same relative price level across all departments—a view not supported by reality. Twenty-three of the 29 supermarkets studied were above average in price in some departments and below average in others (Table 7). This result is based upon a division of supermarkets into only four departments: fresh produce, fresh meats, dry groceries, and non-food. When finer

TABLE 7
PRICE VARIABILITY AMONG DEPARTMENTS
OF THE SAME STORE

Community	No. of Stores with Some Departments Above and Some Below Average	Price Range Among Departments of Same Store	
		Mean	Maximum
Greensboro	3 of 6	6.6	10.5
Havertown	6 of 6	6.2	14.1
New York	2 of 4	6.9	8.6
St. Louis	5 of 6	6.2	12.8
San Francisco	7 of 7	9.1	21.7
TOTAL	23 of 29	7.0[a]	13.5[a]

[a]Averages are calculated giving equal weight to each community.

departmental break-downs are employed, the results show even more departmental variability. The average range among department price indices of a single store (at the same point in time) was 7%, and five stores in the study had a spread in excess of 10%.

The typical "scrambled" pricing strategy is well illustrated by St. Louis departmental price levels. Five of the six supermarkets were above average in some departments and below in others. The average spread was slightly over 6%, and one store had a spread in excess of 12%. The complexity facing the consumer reaches its maximum in San Francisco where the mean spread in departmental prices was 9%.[6]

The average consumer sees every department in the store as a reflection of the overall price level—the well known "halo effect"—even though that view is incorrect. Two-thirds (2/3) of the respondents perceived the same store as the lowest in overall prices, lowest in prices for fresh meats, and lowest in fresh produce. The corresponding statistic for the percentage of respondents placing the same store as the highest in price for all three questions was 60%. Clearly, the consumers do not accurately perceive the extent of differences in a store's prices from department to department.

The halo principle applies regardless of whether or not overall price levels are accurately perceived. Many consumers, having incorrectly placed a particular store as the highest, proceed to place it there for all departments. Interviewers received the general impression that the specific departments named did not determine the response. The shoppers were saying the same store was highest (or lowest) across all departments.

The use of the halo is not uniform across all communities. As shown by Table 8, the percentage of respondents naming the same store as highest (or lowest) on all three questions ranges from 76% in Greensboro to 46% in San Francisco.

Departure from the halo principle does not automatically produce accurate perceptions. The shoppers must recognize which stores are high and which are low in the various departments. San

---

[6]The reliability for the departmental price level measurement is of course less than that for the total market basket index. The non-food department is particularly weak with a sample size of only four. The other departments have sample sizes ranging from 11 to over 40, and in many cases the product price relative is based upon two or more individual items, i.e., two or more brands of the same product were priced.

TABLE 8
PERCENTAGE OF RESPONDENTS USING THE
"HALO PRINCIPLE"

Community	Percentage Using Halo[a]		
	Lowest Priced	Highest Priced	Both Combined
Greensboro	87	66	76
Havertown	69	78	74
New York	64	63	64
St. Louis	57	57	57
San Francisco	55	37	46
TOTAL	66	60	63

[a]Based upon number of respondents who named the same store as lowest (highest) in overall prices, fresh meat prices, and fresh produce prices.

Francisco shoppers were the least likely to rely on a halo, but only 14.2% of their answers for highest (and lowest) stores were correct—against a chance figure of 14.3%.

All five neighborhoods must be classified as inaccurate perceivers of departmental price levels. This classification stems from two principal sources: (1) the view that stores have similar price levels for all departments—the first inaccurate perception, and (2) failure to perceive departmental price levels accurately when attempts are made to discriminate within store price differences.

Magnitude of Price Differences Among Stores

Consumer perceptions of differences among supermarkets' price levels are reasonably good—but only on the average. The median perceived spread for the total study was 8%, compared to an average spread among market basket indices of 5%. In terms of order of magnitude, this average seems like a rather accurate perception.

The five communities show very similar perceived spreads, from a low of 7% to a high of 10% (see Table 9). The spread among market basket indices is much less uniform across neighborhoods, ranging from 2.4% to 7.7%. Perceived spread seems almost independent of market index spread.

Distinct differences in neighborhood accuracy exist for this dimension. Greensboro and New York shoppers show very high accuracy; San Francisco shoppers are very poor; and Havertown and St.

TABLE 9
PERCEIVED SPREAD IN SUPERMARKET PRICE LEVELS
VS. MARKET BASKET INDEX SPREAD

Community	Median Perceived Spread	Market Basket Index Spread
Greensboro	10%	7.5%
Havertown	7%	3.9%
New York	8%	7.7%
St. Louis	7%	3.6%
San Francisco	8%	2.4%
AVERAGE	8%	5.0%

Louis shoppers occupy intermediate positions. These classifications are appropriate for these data, but the haunting thought exists that the perceptions may be generated by a logical construct without regard for the specific environment. If this be true, perceptual accuracy results as a coincidence and not from perceptual ability or discernment.

Price Variability for Specific Products

Consumers in every neighborhood have accurate perceptions of which products are the most stable in price. However, they have much less accurate perceptions of the actual size and frequency of price changes. They greatly understate the extent of price differences among stores, but they perceive within-store price fluctuations more accurately.

The data in Table 10 summarize the perceptions of shoppers concerning price variability for five products identified by the respondents as important in their food purchases—eggs, ground beef, steak, sugar, and milk. Respondents in each neighborhood identified steak (specified as to cut by the individual respondent) as the product with greatest price variability and milk as the product with least variability. These were accurate perceptions in each neighborhood— both when analyzed for price differences among competing super- markets on the same day and when analyzed for within store price fluctuations over a three week interval. The other three products were roughly equivalent to each other in variability for both perceptions and actual prices.

Respondents greatly understate the extent of price differences among stores on the same date. Except for milk, the competing supermarkets rarely charge the same price for a product. Often three or

TABLE 10
PERCEIVED PRICE VARIABILITY OF SPECIFIC PRODUCTS

Product[c]	Across Stores[a]		Across Time[b]	
	Mean Range	% Stating No Difference	Mean Range	% Stating No Difference
Steak (lb.)	10.1¢	22	16.5¢	29
Ground Beef (lb.)	5.7	27	7.8	37
Eggs (doz.)	3.7	30	7.3	29
Sugar (5 lb.)	2.8	54	7.3	46
Milk (½ gal.)[d]	0.6	74	0.6	77

[a]Respondents were asked to specify the typical difference that would exist among the supermarkets of the neighborhood on the same day. The comparison was for the precise item named by the respondent, e.g., sirloin steak, grade A large eggs, ground round, etc.

[b]Respondents were asked to estimate the highest and lowest price for the named item at their regular store during the preceding three weeks.

[c]Respondents were asked to select the five most important products from a list of 11. Others on the list were instant coffee, bananas, fruit punch, lettuce, green peas, and paper towels. Watermelon was added to the list in two communities. The five analyzed in this section are the five chosen by the largest number of respondents.

[d]The average figures for milk combine figures that are not for the same size in all communities. New York and Greensboro respondents specified one quart more often than ½ gallon.

four different prices are charged. The range perceived by customers within a neighborhood is usually about half the range that actually exists.[7] This type of misperception is uniform for all neighborhoods.

Shoppers perceive the price changes within a store with considerable accuracy. The mean ranges across time (column 4 of Table 10) are within 20% of the true figures for each of the products. San Francisco shoppers show some tendency to overstate the size of these price differences, being particularly out of line for sugar.

These two comparisons of price variability for specific products have buying strategy overtones. Will a shopper gain more by proper timing within a particular store or by choosing the right store on any

[7]The average ratio (perceived range to reality range) for the five products over the five neighborhoods was 54%, never rising above 70% for any product except milk.

given day? With the exception of milk, shoppers believe the differences are larger within the same store across time (column 4 vs. column 2)—twice as much for eggs, more than double for sugar, and 1/3 to 2/3 more for ground beef and steak (practically no difference for milk). These differences are just not true! Price variability is almost identical for the two concepts—among stores on the same day and within one store over time. Only New York shoppers recognize this near equality; shoppers in the other four neighborhoods share the misperception.

An element of cognitive dissonance plus a distortion of the time horizon may be at work here. First, the continuous monitoring of a number of stores is time consuming. If the shopper can convince herself that it is unnecessary, she can avoid much extra work and effort. Since most customers shop at the same store on a "regular" basis and fewer than 1% shop at more than two stores, they have good reason for rationalizing equality of price across stores. Second, all stores run specials and occasionally very large price cuts occur. If a store promotes wisely, it can create an image of frequent and deep price reductions on many items. The regular patron recalls some of these large reductions. She has perhaps built her expenditure pattern around the specials and misperceives the frequency of such large reductions. It would be easy to exaggerate the frequency and magnitude of price changes for a product like steak. The price for at least one cut is almost always changing although any specific cut may remain constant in price for several weeks.

SUMMARY

The empirical research demonstrates considerable variation in the accuracy of price perceptions. This variation can be seen through two types of comparisons: (1) perceptual accuracy differs among neighborhoods for any specific dimension of food prices and (2) perceptual accuracy differs within neighborhoods for different dimensions of food prices. The findings indicate that broad statements concerning the accuracy of housewives' price perceptions are unjustified. Misperceptions exist but meaningful conclusions must refer to specific aspects of price perceptions and specific environments.

Perceptions of the overall price levels of competing stores within a neighborhood vary from high accuracy in two communities to a complete lack of accuracy in two others. Complex environments marked by confusing cues and limited variability among alternatives typified the neighborhoods with inaccurate perceptions. The principal cues employed were (1) higher operating expenses will be reflected in higher price levels and (2) large volume operations will be associated with lower prices. Any cue that is intuitively appealing and/or has general accuracy may mislead in specific situations. The evidence suggests that substitution of the expense cue for reality prices contributed to misperceptions in several neighborhoods.

Neighborhood accuracy for overall store price levels is not necessarily a good indicator of perceptual accuracy for other price dimensions. For example, New York shoppers recorded moderate perceptual accuracy for overall supermarket price levels but very low accuracy in their appraisal of small store price levels. Their perceptions of differences among store prices for identical items were more accurate than the perceptions of shoppers in any other neighborhood. No neighborhood was uniformly at the top or bottom in perceptual accuracy for all dimensions.

Finally there are dimensions for which all neighborhoods recorded generally accurate perceptions and others for which perceptions were uniformly inaccurate. All neighborhoods correctly ranked the products with greatest price variability and those with the least variability. The least accurate perceptions existed with respect to the amount of variation among competing stores for the same item—shoppers uniformly understating this figure.

The empirical results demonstrate two conclusions that go beyond the realm of price perceptions for food stores. First, they demonstrate that the general methodological approach employed in this study is feasible. Operational definitions for both reality and perception are needed in order to extend the approach into other areas, but cumulative work over time should yield successively better approximations. Second, the results demonstrate that perception is not identical to reality and the differences may be large. Misallocation of resources could easily stem from these misperceptions—particularly since they seem to be reinforcing rather than offsetting.

Chapter IV

WHICH TYPES OF STORES
ARE MISPERCEIVED?

Consumers have substantial misperceptions of the price levels for over 25% of the supermarkets studied. Defining a "substantial misperception" as a difference between perceived price and market basket index of one standard deviation or more, there is an equal number of stores perceived as higher in price than they really are and stores perceived as lower in price than they really are. In every instance, the perceived price level for the store is consistent with external cues. A store that gives the appearance of having a low cost operation is perceived as lower in price than its market basket index warrants, and a store that appears to have a high cost operation, is perceived as higher in price.

Shoppers show a strong tendency to place stores in a price category—with as little investigation of specific prices as possible. For example, they state that stores belonging to the same chain and within the same neighborhood have identical prices on all items. A particular store of a chain could thus be classified with respect to price without the respondent having checked a single price within that store. There is even some tendency to classify stores of a chain regardless of community. "Chain A is low in prices in every community," according to several respondents. The same tendency appears in appraising stores with common characteristics, but it is strongest where the name is the same.

CHAIN PRICES VERSUS STORE PRICES

Every respondent in the survey rates prices for stores of the same chain as identical—at least within the same neighborhood.[1] Several thought the question ridiculous, believing it obvious that identical prices are

[1] The data presented here refer only to differences within a neighborhood. They should not be compared to views expressed by consumer protection advocates concerning ghetto versus non-ghetto prices.

charged. The evidence does not support this view. Stores within the same chain charge different prices for the same market basket item over 20% of the time.[2]

Differential prices by stores of the same chain show a tendency to offset each other, but they do not completely balance. The Havertown data for the same chain show one store higher for eight items and the other higher for seven. The Greensboro division is nine and seven. The market basket indices differ by 1¼% and 2¼%, a good portion of the index difference resulting from substantial variations in the prices of a few heavily weighted meat items.

Every respondent in these two communities states that stores of the same chain charge the same prices. They do *not* believe, however, that all stores of a chain are identical on *non-price* characteristics. For example, one of the two outlets in Havertown is considered low on cleanliness by a number of respondents. This does not carry over to the second store. In Greensboro, quality and friendliness are rated significantly different for the two stores.

There is some indication that the price level of a chain is imputed across community lines. A portion of this may be a more general perception of lower price levels for large regional and national chains. This tendency is shown by Figure 1 which reveals that seven of eight national and regional chain outlets are perceived as lower in price than reality warrants (below the solid diagonal line).

The figure also reveals that reality price levels for a particular chain are somewhat consistent across communities. Among these eight stores, the four lowest in prices are all from Chain A; the next two are from B; and the two highest are from C. This finding gives some support to the respondents who think a chain's price level is consistent for a broad geographic area. However, the dispersion in Figure 1 shows an element of geographic differences.

Perceptions are a mixture of reality and chain image. Store A_4 benefits from the low price reality and overall image of the entire chain. As an individual store, it is a little above average in market basket index

[2]Two different stores from the same chain were studied in Greensboro, and two stores from another chain were studied in Havertown. Obviously this is a very small sample, but the high frequency of different prices suggests that we are not dealing with isolated instances. The figures were 22% in Havertown and 23% in Greensboro.

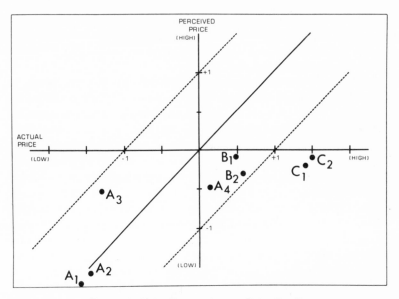

Figure 1. Price Perception vs. Price Reality,
National and Regional Chain Stores.

but is perceived as below average. A_3 is perceived at about the same level as A_4 but charges substantially lower prices.[3]

The four stores from Chains B and C are perceived as slightly below average in prices. This image is not justified for either chain, but it is grossly erroneous for Chain C which has the highest priced stores in each of the neighborhoods in which the chain was studied. The high volume cue to lower prices apparently works for a total organization as well as for an individual store.

MISPERCEPTIONS OF INDIVIDUAL STORES

Three factors contribute to distortions of store price levels: the impression of high (or low) expenses, the appearance of rapid (or slow)

[3] A_3 is the only store for a national or regional chain whose price perception is higher than its price reality. It is not classified as a "misperceived" store in the next section because the difference between perception and reality did not qualify as "substantial."

turnover, and unusually high (or low) quality levels. No stores in Greensboro or Havertown were misperceived to any appreciable extent, reflecting the consistency between these cues and market basket indices for these stores.

Table 1 presents summary information for the eight supermarkets with the largest misperceptions—four perceived as offering lower prices than they really did (negative signs in column 2) and four perceived as charging higher prices than they really did (positive signs). In each case, the store's perceived price has been pulled away from its market index in the direction of these cues—quality, service, or chain membership. In no case is any of these cues in the opposite direction from the misperception.

The highest priced stores in New York, San Francisco, and St. Louis (F, G and H) succeed in establishing much lower price images. Store G is well below average in a number of extra services offered and is not at the top in perceived quality. This store is, therefore, perceived as charging much lower prices than it actually does. Stores F and H are members of a large chain and are also thought to offer low quality. The

TABLE 1
CUES FOR STORE MISPERCEPTIONS

Store[a]	Size of Misperception[b]	Price Rank[c]		Perceived Quality Rank[c]	No. of Services Rank[c]	National or Regional Chain
		Market Basket	Perceived			
A	+1.70	1 (6)	4	4	2	No
B	+1.30	2 (7)	6	7	7	No
C	+1.25	2 (6)	6	6	6	No
D	+1.05	1 (7)	2	6	2	No
E	-1.05	3 (7)	1	3	1	No
F	-1.50	4 (4)	2	1	N.A.	Yes
G	-1.85	7 (7)	3	6	2	No
H	-2.05	6 (6)	3	2	5	Yes

[a]Stores A, C, and H are from St. Louis; Stores B, D, E, and G are from San Francisco; and Store F is from New York.

[b]Misperception is calculated in standard scores as Perceived Price minus Market Basket Index. Plus (+) indicates a store that was perceived as higher in price than it really was. Only stores with differences of 1.00 or more are listed.

[c]Number of supermarkets in the neighborhood is shown in parentheses. All ranks run from low to high, i.e., "1" means lowest in rank whether for price, quality, or service.

result is a low price image.[4] Store E is an average priced store offering the lowest level of services. Respondents inferred a low price level from this lack of services, ranking store E as the lowest of the neighborhood in price as well as services.

The two lowest priced stores in both St. Louis and San Francisco offer quality and service well above that expected from a low priced store. These cues are interpreted as evidence of somewhat higher price levels. Stores B and C are rated as tops in both quality and service. The price perceptions resulting from these cues place C as the highest of its neighborhood and B as the second highest of its neighborhood. Stores A and D are not rated as consistently high on quality and service, but their price perceptions are raised significantly above price reality by these cues.

The evidence in Table 1 shows the quality cue is more influential in St. Louis (Stores A, C and H) while the service cue is more important in San Francisco (Stores B, D, E and G). The perceived price rank for each of these seven stores is within one of the rank on the specified cue. This result is further shown by the rank correlations of .83 in San Francisco (against services) and .44 in St. Louis (against quality).

The rank for both perceived quality and number of services is higher than the market basket index rank wherever price perception is too high. The reverse relationship—quality and service rank lower than the market index—exists for stores perceived lower in price than is warranted.[5] The extent of distortion does not conform to a simple model, but the direction is consistent for all eight stores.

Why Different Cues?

Do these results mean that St. Louis shoppers are more concerned with quality and San Francisco shoppers more concerned with services? We do not believe shoppers make this distinction.

Shoppers are most conscious of those cues which differentiate among the stores of their neighborhood. Every supermarket studied in

[4]One must not conclude that a low price image is necessarily beneficial to the store. Patronage may or may not be associated with price image which is but one of many factors. As we will show in Chapter VI, there is no consistent relationship between patronage and price image for the five neighborhoods studied.

[5]Store E presents a slight modification to this generalization since it occupies the same rank (third) in reality price and perceived quality. It ranks lowest in services, and the resulting perceived price is also lowest.

San Francisco offers parcel carrying and check cashing along with the typical departments, including fresh meat and fresh produce. One store, which is average in prices, offers only these extras. In contrast to this lower limit of four extra services and specialized departments, another store offers 12 extras. A cue is most likely to be operative when competing stores show significant differences in offerings.

The generality of this principle is shown by respondents' classifications of the expenses and price effects of advertising, trading stamps, and modern fixtures. Shoppers were asked to estimate which of these three expenditures cost a store the most and which cost a store the least. They were then asked to estimate the effect each expenditure had on prices—whether it raised, lowered, or had no effect on prices.

Shoppers clearly view advertising as the most expensive of these three items (see Table 2). Over 60% of the respondents rated it as the most costly, and it was considered the most expensive by respondents of each neighborhood. Trading stamps were ranked as the least expensive in each community.

Trading stamps are believed to have the greatest impact on prices despite their perceived lowest cost—almost 3/4 of the respondents think stamps produce higher prices. In contrast, more respondents think modern fixtures and advertising lower prices than think they raise prices. Probing disclosed that these two expenditures fit into the high volume/efficiency cue. Shoppers believe that stores with these characteristics operate on high turnover and low margins, keeping prices relatively low to the consumer. This is not the terminology of the shopper, but it is the fairly sophisticated model employed.

TABLE 2
THE PERCEIVED EFFECT OF
STORE EXPENDITURES ON PRICES

	Percentage Who Believe Expenditure[a]			
Expenditure	*Raises Prices*	*Has No Effect*	*Lowers Prices*	*Costs the Most*
Advertising	40	16	44	62
Modern Fixtures	43	2	55	27
Trading Stamps	73	3	24	11

[a]See Question 25 of the questionnaire for the precise wording of the questions.

Trading stamps are a vastly different kind of expenditure. They represent, in the shopper's eyes, a differential cost to specific stores. They are not considered a high volume/efficiency cue but are placed in this different category.

Shoppers may consider advertising and modern fixtures as expenses common to all supermarkets. In this view, no differential impact on prices should result. Trading stamps are not given by all competing stores. If the shopper believes they represent a differential expense, she believes they will produce a differential price. The potential impact of any cue thus depends on which expenditures are common to the specific environment.

The lowest priced store in both New York and Greensboro was a small store. Only one respondent from each neighborhood correctly perceived this phenomenon. The overriding cue, "small stores are high in price," generated this misperception by most of the respondents.

The power of a name was evidenced in one community. In that community, Discount Food Store (name disguised) had a market basket index 5½% above the supermarket average and almost 10% above the lowest supermarket. Despite this substantial differential, a dozen respondents out of 50—perhaps misled by the name—said it was the lowest priced store of the neighborhood. These respondents represent almost half of the cases in which a small store was classified as the lowest priced store of an entire neighborhood.

MISPERCEPTIONS OF DEPARTMENTAL PRICES

Shoppers create for themselves generalizations of price levels from two possible directions. (1) They form store-wide perceptions and apply them to all departments. (2) They form perceptions of a specific department and impose these perceptions upon the other departments and the total store. Either process runs the risk of generating misperceptions.

Greensboro shoppers correctly perceive both the highest priced and lowest priced store—in overall price levels. They rate these same stores as having the highest and lowest prices in fresh meat and fresh produce as well. These perceptions are accurate for the meat department but not for the produce department. The most expensive store for produce is not greatly misperceived; it is ranked second highest. But the store with the least expensive produce prices is perceived as almost as high as the store that is really the highest. The halo effect is once more in evidence: since the overall rating for this store's prices is well above average, it does not receive proper credit for specific departmental low prices.

The reverse reasoning is illustrated in San Francisco. Consumers have accurate perceptions of the highest priced store for fresh produce. They also place this store highest or second highest for meat prices and overall prices. They are grossly incorrect in the latter instances. This store is the lowest priced store for fresh meat and next to the lowest in overall prices. In this instance, the shopper's accurate perception for a specific department has been generalized—without justification—to other parts of the store.

The limited data suggest that a strong halo effect exists in price and only slightly less in quality. The same store was perceived as the highest (or lowest) priced store for fresh meat, fresh produce, and overall in eight of ten cases. Quality perceptions for highest or lowest were identical in six of ten instances.[6]

SUMMARY

We can place individual stores in three different categories with respect to the accuracy of their price perceptions: those whose prices are lower than the shoppers realize, those whose prices are higher than the shoppers realize, and those whose prices are perceived accurately. Most stores' price levels are validly perceived, but significant distortions exist for a substantial minority—eight of 29 supermarkets in this study. An equal division—rather than an imbalance—seems to exist between the number of stores for which price levels are understated and the number for which price levels are overstated.

Shoppers seem to substitute readily observed cues and operating characteristics for factual price data when they form misperceptions. They classify stores according to these characteristics, and they assign the price level associated with the characteristics. The more these cues fit together, the more difficult it is for the store to escape the

[6]Quality ratings were obtained for only two departments (fresh meat and fresh produce). No overall quality level was obtained except that calculated as an average of the two departments. It would, of course, be inappropriate to use that average as a third measure in testing for consistency.

image—regardless of its true price level. The ultimate cue creating a specific price image is membership in the same chain, particularly for stores of the chain in close geographic proximity.

Shoppers normally form accurate perceptions if a store's price level is consistent with the cues. A store is inviting misperception if its pricing policies are at variance with its principal non-price operating policies. The cues with the greatest impact on price perception are quality levels, services offered, unusual departments, size of store, and size of total organization. Heterogeneity of the environment in a specific factor magnifies the impact of that factor, and homogeneity of the environment for the factor dampens its salience.

These results reinforce the findings of the previous chapter. Shoppers perceive that a store with higher expenses than its competitors will also be higher in price. They perceive that a big volume operation will have lower prices than its competitors. These tendencies appear regardless of the actual price levels of a store. In some cases, the resulting perceptions are accurate; but in others, they are inaccurate.

Chapter V

INDIVIDUAL SHOPPERS DIFFER
IN PERCEPTUAL ACCURACY

Every community has some shoppers whose price perceptions are almost prefectly accurate. Simultaneously, each has other shoppers whose perceptions are grossly inaccurate. Reasons for these individual differences are easy to hypothesize, varying from shopping behavior and shopping attitudes to socio-economic and personality characteristics. The empirical results concerning explanatory variables are inconclusive and fragmentary but offer a beginning.

A partial reason for the inconclusive results in explaining why some shoppers perceive accurately is provided by the individual shopper's inconsistency. A housewife who accurately perceives that a particular small store is low in prices may have inaccurate perceptions concerning the relative price levels among the competing supermarkets. Another housewife who perceives the relative price levels of the supermarkets accurately may misperceive differences in departmental price levels.

Shoppers in different neighborhoods can realize widely different payoffs from accurate perceptions, depending on the amount of variability among alternatives. Different ranges among stores in price reality also produce two conflicting and paradoxical tendencies.

1. Large differences in price realities make it easier for shoppers to form accurate price perceptions.

2. These same large differences produce large economic losses if misperception occurs.

If small differences exist in price reality, shoppers are less likely to have accurate perceptions; but the probability that they will experience large economic losses due to misperceptions is small.

DIFFERENCES AMONG SHOPPERS IN PERCEPTUAL ACCURACY

Wide differences exist in the perceptual accuracy of shoppers within the same neighborhood. The best perceivers are at least 70% and perhaps

TABLE 1
DIFFERENCE IN PERCEPTUAL ACCURACY AMONG
SHOPPERS OF THE SAME NEIGHBORHOOD

Community	Superiority of Best Perceivers Over Worst[a]	% of Inaccurate Perceivers[b]	% of Excellent Perceivers[c]
Greensboro	96%	18	24
Havertown	94	7	34
New York	83	35	8
St. Louis	71	73	1
San Francisco	81	46	5

[a]Superiority is computed by comparing the tenth and ninetieth percentile scores.

[b]An inaccurate perceiver is defined as one whose perceptual accuracy score is worse than a randomly derived score.

[c]An excellent perceiver is defined as one whose perceptual accuracy score is 75% better than a randomly derived score.

over 90% better than the worst perceivers. Some shoppers within any given neighborhood would record better perceptions if they drew answers at random while others have very high accuracy—over 60 of our 1000 plus shoppers place their neighborhood supermarkets in perfect rank order.

Table 1 shows the extent of variability among shoppers of each neighborhood.[1] Even in St. Louis where only 1% of the respondents record excellent perceptions (that is, 75% improvement over chance), the upper tenth in perception is 71% better than the lower tenth. In Greensboro and Havertown, the best perceivers are about 95% better than the worst. These figures would, of course, be even higher if more extreme values were used in defining the best and worst perceivers.

The table also establishes that each neighborhood has some excellent perceivers and some very poor perceivers although the relative number of each varies greatly. This division is the dominant factor in determining the overall accuracy of neighborhood perceptions. The large proportion of inaccurate perceivers in St. Louis and San Francisco

[1]As was discussed in Chapter II, we believe the classification of individuals in perceptual accuracy is more tenuous than it is for individual stores or for the total neighborhood. Despite this reservation, we believe the measures employed in classifying individuals are the best available at the present time. Consequently they will be used without elaborate qualifications throughout the discussion.

(and the small proportion of excellent perceivers) produces the inaccurate aggregate ratings of these communities. The contrasting pattern of Greensboro and Havertown yield their overall accurate perceptions. Despite these differences among communities in the relative sizes of the two groups of respondents, the differences in perceptual accuracy within each community are substantial.

EXPLANATIONS FOR INDIVIDUAL DIFFERENCES IN ACCURACY

We can easily hypothesize why shoppers differ in the accuracy of their price perceptions. Some shoppers devote much time and effort to the task; some put great stress on price; some have recently moved to the neighborhood while others are well established. These are but a few of the variables that might logically be related to the formation of accurate perceptions. Most of the empirical evidence is consistent with these intuitions, but the weakness of the relationships is disappointing.

Twenty-four different characteristics were tested as potential explanatory variables for perceptual accuracy. No single variable accounted for as much as 5% of the variance in perceptual accuracy within any community, and the maximum for all variables combined was 12%.[2]

Shopping attitudes and shopping behavior show stronger relations with perceptual accuracy than do socio-economic variables such as income, education, and job status. Although they show stronger relationships, the shopping characteristics are less consistent and may be more closely related to store cues and consensus views than to the accuracy of perceptions. The socio-economic variables are more consistent across communities, but the associations are extremely weak.

Patronage Versus Perceptual Accuracy

Regular patrons of the lowest priced stores have the most accurate price perceptions. Conversely, patrons of the highest priced stores have the least accurate price perceptions.

The more accurate perceptions by the patrons of low priced stores are shown in Table 2. Regular patrons of the lowest priced store

[2]See Appendix G and Appendix H for descriptions of the specific variables, various transformations, and the types of regression equations used. The 12% refers to the step-wise equation with a limited number of independent variables, not the total equation with all variables.

TABLE 2
PERCEPTUAL ACCURACY VERSUS PRICE LEVEL
FOR STORE PATRONIZED REGULARLY

Price Rank of Store (Low to High)	Perceptual Accuracy Rank of Regular Patrons[a]				
	Greensboro	Havertown	New York	St. Louis	San Francisco
1	1	1	2	2	1
2	2	2	1	3	4
3	3	3	3	1	2
4	4		4	4	3
5				5	
6				6	

[a]Includes only stores with more than 10 regular patrons in sample.

have the most accurate perceptions in three communities and the second most accurate in the other two communities. Patrons of the highest priced store are the least accurate perceivers in four cities and only slightly better in the fifth.

These results show perceptual accuracy for patrons of low priced stores, but it is not clear that the results stem from perceptual ability. Shoppers may simply rationalize their preference and by coincidence record more accurate perceptions.

Many shoppers show a tendency to rank the store they shop regularly as lower in price than its price index warrants. This downward bias produces misperceptions for all shoppers except those who actually patronize the lowest priced store. It is impossible for patrons of the lowest priced store to assign it a ranking below "lowest." Therefore, any downward bias by these patrons would not show misperceptions in an ordinal ranking system.[3]

This manifestation of cognitive dissonance handicaps the consumer's perceptual process and simultaneously presents the store a unique opportunity in dealing with its current customers. The store can reinforce and strengthen existing favorable dispositions by offering selected price reductions. Even if the number of reductions is small, present customers will generalize to other products because they are anxious to believe the prices are low. The housewife who wishes to

[3]Interval ratings, requiring the respondent to state "how much lower," would overcome this problem.

form accurate perceptions must guard against this temptation to generalize from a biased selection of items.

Which Variables Best Explain Accurate Perceptions?

Motivation, specific experience, general abilities, and effort should contribute to superior performance in any undertaking. A major research problem arises when we try to identify appropriate indicators for each of these factors and attempt to isolate the effect of each more narrowly defined indicator.

Motivation for forming accurate perceptions of food prices may be evidenced by such items as interest in food shopping, satisfaction in doing a good job, and financial constraints. Each is a motivating factor of a different type, but each should logically contribute to more accurate perceptions.

Specific experience in food shopping is shown by frequency of shopping trips, length of residence in the specific neighborhood, number of different stores visited, and number of years the shopper has been the principal food buyer for household. The appropriate types of exposures and the proper measurements must be settled in a rather arbitrary manner. Those chosen for this study reflect heavy weights on interview feasibility and communication ease, rather than on a thorough theoretical model.

General perceptual abilities are shown by mental capabilities and cultural or business awareness. Education is the best example in the present study. Sex, marital status, employment status, and age might have certain overtones for general abilities; but their inclusion in this category is debatable.

Effort is related to specific experience and motivation, but it must be demonstrated through purposeful activity. In this particular research, our measures of effort must refer to the formation of accurate perceptions. Search activity, price concern, and pre-purchase planning are all illustrative of such effort.

The specific variables we tested support the preceding arguments. Housewives with more accurate price perceptions exert greater effort in food shopping, have more interest in it, have more experience with food shopping, have greater motivation, and have richer cultural backgrounds. These patterns emerged in 2/3 of the tests we performed (see Table 3). The relationships are not strong. There are many

TABLE 3
FACTORS ASSOCIATED WITH PERCEPTUAL ACCURACY

Factor[a]	No. of Tests[b]	Percentage Showing Positive Relations
Motivation	35	66
Shopping Experience	25	68
Shopping Effort	25	68
General Abilities	15	80
TOTAL	80[c]	66

[a]Classification of specific variables into the four factors was arbitrary. Some variables were assigned to more than one factor, and others were not included in any of these four. Different bases of classification are employed in Table 4. The precise questions and their assignment are shown in Appendix G.

[b]Each variable was tested in each of five communities.

[c]Variables assigned to more than one factor are counted only once in the total. Those assigned to more than one factor were more likely to show positive relations.

inconsistencies, but the data sketch the beginnings of an explanatory model.

Specific shopping variables are more closely associated with perceptual accuracy than are more general variables. Paradoxically the specific variables are less consistent across communities. The first variable entering the step-wise equation[4] is a shopping variable for four communities, and nine of the thirteen variables (in the step-wise equations) are in the shopping category. Shopping in different stores, shopping for price, and normal use of a shopping list are among the better indicators of perceptual accuracy—each appearing in more than one community.

No variable accounts for as much as 5% of the variance in perceptual accuracy, and the total equation reaches a maximum value of only .12 (R^2 in Greensboro). Even when all 20 variables were

[4]Strength of relationship is best shown by the step-wise regression results. Variables are added to the equation as long as the F ratio for the new variable is significant at the .05 level. The BMD-02R program was used for these equations.

TABLE 4
CONSISTENCY OF RELATIONSHIPS BETWEEN PERCEPTUAL
ACCURACY AND SHOPPER CHARACTERISTICS

| Type Variable | No. Tested | No. Consistent in 4 or 5 Communities | |
		Observed[a]	Theoretical[b]
Socio-Economic	7	6[c]	2.625
Shopping Attitudes	5	3	1.875
Shopping Behavior	8	2	3.000
TOTAL	20	11	7.500

[a]The specific variables showing consistency are: (1) Socio-economic—sex, marital status, income, full-time employment, part-time employment, and tenure/age; (2) Shopping attitudes—opinion of others' shopping ability, concern for price, and opinion of own shopping ability; and (3) Shopping behavior—shop by auto and order size/household composition. The precise questions employed are shown in Appendix G.

[b]Theoretical calculation is based on $(\frac{1}{2} + \frac{1}{2})^5$. The probability of 4 or 5 communities having the same sign is 3/8. 3/8 times the number of variables = theoretical.

[c]Significantly higher than theoretical (.05 level of significance). Based on $(3/8 + 5/8)^n$ where n = number of variables.

included in the regression equations, the R^2 value never reaches .20, thus leaving over 80% of the variance unexplained.

Socio-economic variables show greater consistency in their relationships to accurate perceptions than do the shopping variables. Two of the seven socio-economic variables reveal the same relationship in every community, and four others show consistency for four communities. As shown in Table 4, this figure of six out of seven is more than double the theoretical number expected from chance alone. The results for both types of shopping variables vary across communities, suggesting that their effects depend upon the specific environment.[5]

The data do not justify the building of an elaborate model to explain which shoppers perceive food prices most accurately. However, several general observations are appropriate.

[5] A null hypothesis of independence of signs among communities would be accepted for both types of shopping variables but rejected for the socio-economic (.05 level of significance). Exact probabilities for the binomial were used for the test (see Table 4).

1. The inconsistency of the relationships between shopping variables and perceptual accuracy suggests that interest in and concern for shopping may make consumers cognizant of cues, store policies, and consensus opinions—and not necessarily contribute to accurate price perceptions.

2. The formation of price perceptions may depend on very specific activities. Shopping behavior and shopping attitudes yield stronger relationships than general socio-economic characteristics. Perhaps even stronger relationships exist with questions that are more specific and detailed than those used in this study.

3. Great care should be exercised to distinguish between variables that explain the formation of *perceptions* and those that explain the formation of *accurate perceptions.* They are related but far from identical.

The formation of accurate perceptions is difficult. Confusing and contradictory evidence abounds. General cultural awareness and mental capacities are prerequisites, but alone they contribute little to the formation of accurate perceptions for any particular phenomenon. General abilities must be applied through the allocation of attention, the processing of sensory data, and accurate retention and recall—to name only the main points. The formation of perceptions is a very complex process, and we believe the accuracy of perceptions depends mainly on the specifics of the problem. These specifics include the external or environmental reality that is to be perceived, but they also include the internal state of the perceiver. To complicate the problem even more, the internal state of the perceiver is composed of her transitory conditions at any given moment as well as her more abiding characteristics.[6]

The Role of Individual Variables

Certain individual variables within the various categories reveal consistency across communities. Several of the results are contrary to our *a priori* hypotheses, but with 20/20 hindsight they seem reasonable.

The married full-time housewife is not a valid perceiver of food prices. This conclusion is supported by four different variables. Male food shoppers are more accurate perceivers of price than female food shoppers. Single shoppers are better perceivers than their married

---

[6]Chapter VII discusses the perceptual process in much more detail, particularly as it pertains to this project.

counterparts. Part-time employees perceive prices more accurately than those not employed, and full-time employees have more accurate perceptions than part-time employees.

The food purchasing agent of a household is normally female—approximately 90% of our shoppers are women. The male food shopper is the exception and has probably chosen the task. The female food shopper may be forced into the task, thus having less interest in the drab, mundane, and even trivial chore. The higher interest and motivation by the male shopper may explain his more accurate perceptions.

The employed and single shoppers may be under greater time and financial constraints. Leisurely shopping is a luxury they cannot afford; efficiency is required. More accurate perceptions are demanded and more likely to result.

Higher income has elements of achievement, ability, and cultural awareness which should contribute to more accurate perceptions; but it also connotes less financial need to perceive accurately. Ability is a prerequisite for accurate perceptions; need cannot be met without ability. Income is positively associated with more accurate perceptions in each of the five communities, suggesting that income shows ability more than financial need and motivation.

The income results dramatize the position of social critics and consumer protection advocates. Those who can least afford the cost of misperceptions—those who should be most concerned with price—are the most likely to misperceive.

Older age, longer residence in the neighborhood, larger household size, and children within the household are all positively associated with more accurate perceptions. Some of these factors are partial indicators of need and fortunately show the reverse of the income result; in these cases, persons with the greatest need are more likely to form accurate price perceptions. There is some suggestion that the age/tenure configuration has a curvilinear relation to accuracy with the most accurate perceivers 45-55 years old and having 3-5 years of residence in the neighborhood.[7]

The shopping variables showing the most consistency are concern for prices, amount of search effort, appraisal of self as a shopper, use of

---

[7]If this is true, a curvilinear fitting would show the variables as even more important. More precision than is employed in the present questionnaire would be needed to test for non-linearity.

auto in shopping, and appraisal of other shoppers. Price concern is consistently related to accurate price perceptions in all five neighborhoods and shows the strongest relationship of all variables studied.[8] Search effort is intuitively appealing, and it is reassuring to find it associated with more accurate perceptions.

A critical attitude of one's own shopping ability and a similarly critical attitude of others' abilities seem to produce greater accuracy. Shoppers who are less confident of their own ability and more critical of others may be more aware of the complex nature of food price patterns. Their counterparts may incorrectly think the patterns are quite simple.

Auto use in shopping is the last shopping variable showing consistent results. Shopping by auto is associated with more accurate perceptions and may simply reflect a wider exposure to the environment.

Frequency of shopping, regular shopping at more than one store, satisfaction from shopping, preparation of a list prior to shopping, and education reveal no consistent patterns. The amount and kind of shopping experience should logically relate to the decision under investigation. Exposure to relevant options should help in the deliberations and the formation of accurate perceptions. Future investigations should focus on more specific explanatory variables than those in the present study and should pursue them in greater depth.

INCONSISTENCY OF INDIVIDUALS IN PERCEPTUAL ACCURACY

General characteristics do not assure accurate perceptions; they supply the foundation upon which accurate perceptions may be formed. A shopper who forms accurate perceptions regarding store price levels has the ability to form accurate perceptions for other decisions, but she may fail to use that ability. Accurate perceivers on one price dimension are often inaccurate perceivers on other dimensions.

A shopper may know the relative price levels of competing stores but overstate or understate price changes over time. She may realize the extent of differences among stores for a particular item but not

[8]The regression coefficient for price concern is larger than its own standard error in three communities and more than double in one. The only other variable with coefficients of this magnitude has the wrong sign in two communities. This variable is the use of a shopping list.

perceive that stores occupy different price ranks for different departments. Both of these patterns and many other inconsistencies are the
norm rather than the exception.

Consumers who have a good grasp and understanding of food
store prices should know the approximate range of price levels among
neighborhood supermarkets. Those who place \ this range at less than
1% or at 20-25% are clearly in error. We estimate that slightly less than
half of the consumers perceive this dimension accurately (44% as shown
in Table 5).[9] Accuracy for this dimension is but weakly related to
accuracy for other dimensions.

The data in Table 5 illustrate the inconsistency with which
individual shoppers form accurate price perceptions. A person who is an
accurate perceiver for one dimension is more likely to be an accurate
perceiver for another dimension, but a large number of individuals are
accurate for one and inaccurate for others.[10] The inconsistency is seen
most clearly by examining the number of individuals in the upper right
and lower left corners of the table. Part A of the table shows that 38%
of the shoppers have accurate perceptions for one dimension and
inaccurate perceptions for the other (21% plus 17%). The same general
inconsistency is seen in Part B of the table where the figure is 40%.

Shoppers who are accurate perceivers of dimensions which are
missed by almost all shoppers might be expected to record accurate
perceptions for the more easily discerned dimensions. For example, a
shopper who is able to perceive that a particular small store is low in
prices should be able to distinguish among the price levels of the
supermarkets. Or a person who knows that the same store is the highest
priced store for meat and simultaneously the lowest for produce ought
to have accurate perceptions of other dimensions. The results indicate
that these individuals are better than average on other dimensions but
not among the very best.

Five persons validly perceived such difficult situations. All five
achieved individual perceptual validity scores (for store selection) better
than the neighborhood average, but none was in the top 10%. Weak

---

[9]The criterion used for an accurate perception was an answer between 2% and
10%.

[10]A null hypothesis of independence would be rejected at the .05 level of
significance for both sections of Table 5.

TABLE 5
SHOPPER CONSISTENCY IN FORMING
ACCURATE PERCEPTIONS FOR
DIFFERENT PRICE DIMENSIONS

A. Magnitude of Range Versus Store Ranks[a]

| | *Store Ranks*[c] | | |
Percentage Range[b]	*Accurate*	*Inaccurate*	*Total*
Accurate	23%	21%	44%
Inaccurate	17%	39%	56%
TOTAL	40%	60%	100%

B. Magnitude of Range Versus Departmental
Differences[a]

| | *Departmental Differences*[d] | | |
Percentage Range[b]	*Accurate*	*Inaccurate*	*Total*
Accurate	17%	27%	44%
Inaccurate	13%	43%	56%
TOTAL	30%	70%	100%

[a]Figures show percentage of respondents in each category.

[b]Shoppers who stated overall price range was between 2% and 10% were classified as accurate; others were classified as inaccurate. Reality indices varied between 7.7% in New York and 2.4% in San Francisco.

[c]Classification for accuracy on store ranks was based upon individual perceptual accuracy scores (see Chapter II). The middle 40% for each neighborhood were classified as valid.

[d]Any respondent who correctly identified (i) the highest priced store for overall prices, (ii) the highest for fresh meat, and (iii) the highest for fresh produce *or* the lowest for all three was classified as accurate for departmental differences.

relationships do exist: shoppers who perceive one price dimension accurately are more likely to perceive other price dimensions accurately. But inconsistency is widespread.

SUMMARY

Some shoppers perceive reality with almost perfect accuracy. Others find the nature of reality an unsolved mystery. These wide differences in perceptual validity exist within every neighborhood, and they exist for every dimension of food prices.

Our attempts to explain differences among individuals in perceptual accuracy met with low levels of success. Socio-economic variables indicate that certain characteristics might be prerequisite to accurate perceptions, but they in no way guarantee perceptual accuracy. These variables incorporate mental capacity, a richer cultural awareness, and some achievement motivation. Their results are consistent across communities but extremely weak. Specific shopping activities and attitudes show somewhat stronger relationships to perceptual accuracy (still explaining less than 20% of the variance) but a lack of consistency across communities.

The same individual may form accurate perceptions for one price dimension and inaccurate perceptions for others. The capacity to form accurate perceptions must be present, but the specific conditions and characteristics that increase perceptual accuracy for specific decisions are unclear.

Individual shopper characteristics react with specific environmental conditions, and these interactions cumulate over time. The weak relationships discovered should not be surprising. Different individuals sense and process different bits of price and non-price data from their environments. Different generalizations are made and serve until revised as bases for decisions. The process is further complicated because different decisions require different types of generalizations.

The complexity of the environment and the complexity of the perceptual process underscore the difficult task facing the individual shopper. A pessimist might say the perceptions formed would be the complete result of chance. An optimist might say a few simple and important factors determine the resulting perceptions. We reject both positions. Certain factors do influence perceptual accuracy, but they seem to be numerous and not easily combined into overall important categories.

Chapter VI

THE ECONOMIC SIGNIFICANCE
OF MISPERCEPTION

The economic significance of misperception depends on the losses suffered because of these misperceptions. If all options are essentially the same, the consequences of non-optimal selection are slight and misperceptions are of small concern. Concerted search effort would not be warranted. If options differ greatly, inaccurate perceptions have substantial economic significance. Considerable search and additional costs would be justified in order to gain accurate perceptions.

The number of relevant options open to a purchaser and the degree of similarity among them differs from one situation to another and from one purchaser to another. The specific data presented in this chapter refer to household purchases of food in five neighborhoods. They represent five case studies at particular points in time. Attempts to generalize to other localities or points in time are suspect even for the food purchase decision—they do not measure the overall economic signficance of misperceptions. These data do illustrate several important points concerning the subject of economic misperceptions.

—The decision maker has several decisions, not just one—he must decide which decisions are worthy of his attention and which are relatively minor.

—The decision maker may stress either the avoidance of large losses or the selection of near optimal decisions.

—The cost of forming accurate perceptions differs considerably for different decision problems.

COMPETING SUPERMARKETS CHARGE DIFFERENT PRICES

Many knowledgeable individuals warned us that our market basket approach (same brand/size for all stores) would show identical prices by all competitors. They reasoned that prices on well known highly visible items would be matched by competitors. This most certainly is not the case!

Identical prices exist for all supermarkets on fewer than 15% of the items. This figure is based on only those items available in every store of the neighborhood on the same day—the items most likely to qualify as well known and highly visible. The products with identical prices throughout a neighborhood are quite dissimilar from city to city. The only products repeated in as many as three cities are American cheese, milk, and Italian salad dressing. Six others show identical prices in two cities, but the remaining 19 cases occur in only one city per product. If small stores are included, identical prices do not exist for any items.

The median number of different prices is three. Table 1 shows the great variation among supermarkets in prices charged for these market basket items. In three cities four different prices are charged more often than a single price, and in every city there is at least one item for which

TABLE 1
NUMBER OF DIFFERENT PRICES CHARGED
FOR IDENTICAL ITEMS

No. of Different Prices	No. of Items[a]				
	Greensboro[b]	Havertown[b]	New York	St. Louis	San Francisco
1	11	5	11	11	2
2	11	13	22	15	8
3	12	18	19	10	8
4	8	12	9	14	12
5	7	5	c	7	6
6	2	5	c	2	6
7	c	c	c	c	1
TOTAL	51	58	61	59	43

[a]Analysis based on only items in stock in all neighborhood supermarkets on same day.

[b]In both Greensboro and Havertown, two of the supermarkets are members of the same chain. The analysis considers each store as a separate entity.

[c]The number of different prices obviously could not exceed the number of stores. The number of supermarkets by city were: Greensboro - 6, Havertown - 6, New York - 4, St. Louis - 6, and San Francisco - 7.

every supermarket has a different price. Uniform prices do not apply, even for the most popular brands and sizes of fast moving items.

Stores within each neighborhood also differ in overall price levels. This is most dramatic if both supermarkets and small stores are included in the comparisons—reaching a range of 30% in Havertown although only 6½% in San Francisco. The spread among supermarkets is considerably less, but reaches over 7% in both New York and Greensboro. Shoppers in San Francisco might be justified in considering the 2½% spread among supermarkets as too small to warrant more than minimal shopping or search effort.

Prices change over time in addition to differing among stores at a point in time. These changes are most obvious for individual items although overall price levels also fluctuate slightly. Most stores change their prices for market basket items at least once a month and much more frequently for fresh products. The resulting changes in market basket indices are usually less than 1% but occasionally a change of 2-3% occurs.

The existence of these various types of price differences opens a host of possible purchase strategies. The wisdom of each and the amount of complexity appropriate depends on the size of these price differences and the ease with which a purchaser could secure current information. These factors and their strategy implications will be explored in the next section of this chapter.

SAVINGS FROM ALTERNATIVE STRATEGIES

Given that competing food stores charge dissimilar prices for many items and have different average price levels, how much can a housewife save by making the proper store selection? How much additional can she save by shopping at two stores? At three? Should the average consumer establish sub-groups of products that she should purchase at specific stores? If she should, what would these sub-groups be and how much would she save? How much can be saved by stocking-up at "specials"? Should purchase strategies be revised periodically? How much is lost if no revision is made? All of these questions are different views of the economic significance of misperception in food purchases.

The payoff from different buying strategies can be measured in many different ways, but we regard three as most reasonable.

1. How much would be saved by following the optimal strategy in contrast to a random choice?

2. How much better is the best strategy than the worst?

3. How much better is a particular strategy than some alternative that might be employed?

In each approach, a strategy is compared to a different base—a purchase decision that might occur if accurate perceptions are lacking.[1] All three will be used as we consider the store selection decision.

Buying Strategy: Choose One Store

The simplest buying strategy available is to choose a single store and purchase all items at that store. More complicated strategies are justified only if they yield greater savings (or greater utility if both price and non-price dimensions are involved).

The relevant payoff matrix for deciding where to purchase the market basket is given by Table 2 (using Havertown as an example). We assume only one store is to be used and the entire market basket is to be purchased. Store A is the best option, but what are the potential savings? Three different measures are given in the table, with answers varying from 1.5% to 3.8%. There is no "correct" measure of the savings available, but the measures can magnify or minimize the apparent savings. By judicious selection, very different impressions can be given. Differences in the measurements of the cost of misperception are even greater—ranging from 1.2% to 4.0%.

The gain from accurate perceptions depends on the shopper's preceding state of ignorance. "No knowledge" would coincide to a random selection on the average, but it might yield the very worst selection. Complete accuracy might, on the other hand, represent only a slight improvement over a previous condition of reasonably good

[1]Formal decision theory permits application of different criteria but does not supply a basis for selecting among criteria. Utility theory uses transformations of monetary results into "utiles" but does not supply the transformation functions. These statements are not meant to disparage these techniques but to point out that they do not specify the appropriate measure. The selection of measurement criteria is idiosyncratic; each buyer must select her own. An alternative approach to the three comparisons presented here would evaluate the possible loss if perceptions were not accurate rather than the savings if they were. Since distributions need not be symmetric, the results may be quite dissimilar.

TABLE 2
SAVINGS FROM ACCURATE PERCEPTIONS, HAVERTOWN SUPERMARKETS

Supermarket	Market Basket Index
A	97.9
B	99.4
C	100.0
D	100.2
E	100.6
F	101.8

SAVINGS POSSIBLE FROM ACCURATE PERCEPTIONS

Lowest Priced vs. Average (97.9 vs. 100.0) = 2.1% Saving
Lowest Priced vs. Highest Priced (97.9 vs. 101.8) = 3.8% Saving
Lowest Priced vs. Second Lowest (97.9 vs. 99.4) = 1.5% Saving

POSSIBLE COSTS OF MISPERCEPTIONS

Highest Priced vs. Average (101.8 vs. 100.0) = 1.8% Cost
Highest Priced vs. Second Highest (101.8 vs. 100.6) = 1.2% Cost
Highest Priced vs. Lowest Priced (101.8 vs. 97.9) = 4.0% Cost

TABLE 3
SAVINGS FROM ACCURATE PERCEPTIONS: CHOOSING THE RIGHT STORE

Community	Potential Savings	
	Low vs. High	Low vs. Average
New York	7.4%	3.6%
Greensboro	7.3	5.0
Boca Raton[a]	6.1	3.1
Brooklyn[a]	5.4	3.0
Havertown	3.8	2.1
St. Louis	3.5	2.0
San Francisco	2.4	1.0
AVERAGE	5.1%	2.8%

[a]Data collected from other research projects on pricing. See footnote 2.

perceptions. We prefer the comparison against random as a less extreme position but recognize its arbitrary nature.

The risks from inaccurate perceptions and the potential savings from accurate perceptions vary considerably among neighborhoods, but the orders of magnitude are roughly the same. The low priced store is approximately 5% lower than the high priced store and about 3% below the average of the neighborhood (see Table 3).[2] San Francisco shoppers can save the least from store selection, less than half the amount available in other neighborhoods. Greensboro shoppers can save the most—50% more than the average figures.

The economic importance of these savings depends upon the size of the order and the financial condition of the household. The typical order size in the five neighborhoods is $20-25, implying a potential saving (based upon low vs. average) of 60 to 75 cents per order. Savings of this magnitude become significant if they can be repeated week after week; otherwise they may be trivial. The data suggest that similar savings can be repeated week after week, but the same store may not always have the lowest prices. If the store to patronize is a decision that once made can be retained for a long period, the savings generated would be significant for most households. If it is accurate for only one shopping trip, its economic value would be slight.[3]

Another question is whether the lowest priced *store* should be identified or whether it is sufficient to identify the lowest priced *stores*. If the lowest priced *store* is just a little cheaper than the next lowest, the consumer does not gain much from knowing which is *the* lowest. Selection of either low priced store would yield approximately the same savings.

The differential between the two lowest priced stores is over 3% in both New York and Greensboro. In the other cities the differential is less than 2%, and it is only ½% in San Francisco.

The big payoff may come from avoiding certain stores. Housewives in New York should know the highest priced store since it is

[2] Supplementary data from Boca Raton, Florida, and Brooklyn, New York, are included throughout this chapter. Only reality price data were obtained in these projects. The Brooklyn figures are for three selected weeks between September 1965 and March 1966. The Boca Raton figures cover five consecutive weeks in the winter of 1968.

[3] This question is considered later in the chapter under "Stability of Optimal Purchasing Strategies." The limited data available suggest that stores do not shift greatly in relative average prices.

almost 4% higher than any other store. In no other case is the difference between the two highest stores as much as 2%.

The shopper must first determine the type of price reality that exists in her neighborhood. Only then does she know whether she should identify *the* low priced store, a *group* of low priced stores, or *the* high priced store. Also, only then does she know whether the formation of accurate perceptions is worth the effort and cost. She might decide to ignore the problem—at the store selection stage. This would seem an appropriate position if savings of 5% or less are trivial to her. But she must also investigate whether more complex strategies will yield even larger savings.

Splitting Purchases Among Stores

The most extreme position a housewife could take for one day's food purchases would be to purchase each separate item from the store offering it at the lowest price that day. Could most of the savings

TABLE 4
SAVINGS ATTAINABLE:
ITEM BY ITEM PURCHASES

| | *Potential Savings* | |
Community	*Over Random*[a]	*Improvement Over Store Selection*[b]
New York	12.1%	3.4
San Francisco	8.8	8.8
St. Louis	8.6	4.3
Boca Raton	8.2	2.6
Greensboro	8.0	1.6
Brooklyn	7.9	2.6
Havertown	5.6	2.6
AVERAGE	**8.4%**	3.0[c]

[a]Lowest possible expenditure for market basket compared to random selection.

[b]Item by item percentage saving $\div$ best single store percentage saving. Both figures are compared against random selection. (Column 2 of Table 4 $\div$ Column 3 of Table 3.)

[c]The 3.0 figure is based on the averages of 8.4% and 2.8% and is not the average of the community ratios.

TABLE 5
SAVINGS FROM DIFFERENT
SHOPPING STRATEGIES[a]

| Number of Stores Shopped | Basis for Combining Products | | |
	Items (No Combinations)[c]	Product Categories[d]	Departments[d]
1	2.8%[e]	2.8%[e]	2.8%[e]
2	6.4	4.6	3.8
3	7.7	5.3	3.9
4[b]	8.1	5.6	3.9

[a]Savings are calculated against a base of random selection.

[b]There are more than four stores in several of the neighborhoods. If all stores are shopped, the savings reach 8.4% for item by item shopping and 5.7% for product category shopping. Since only four departments are defined, departmental shopping is limited to four stores.

[c]Each item is purchased from the store with the lowest price for that item, restricting purchases to no more than the number of stores specified.

[d]Fourteen product categories and four departments are defined. The assignment of products is shown in Appendix D. All products within a product category (or department) are purchased from the store having the lowest total cost for each group.

[e]By definition all products are combined when purchase is from a single store.

attainable from such a complex procedure be realized by much simpler shopping plans? For example, can she shop at only two or three stores instead of six or seven? Can she purchase all products of the same type from a particular store instead of buying on an item by item basis?

Item by item shopping would produce an average saving of 8%—triple the 2.8% attainable by choosing the lowest priced store.[4] The superiority of item by item shopping over shopping at the lowest priced store is not constant among neighborhoods (see Table 4). Such detailed shopping is least warranted where a particular store offers a large price saving, for example, in Greensboro. Even here savings would be increased by 60% (1.6 of column 3). In San Francisco, item shopping savings completely dwarf store selection savings (8.8 times as

[4]Both comparisons are against a random selection. Total savings from item shopping would be over 10% when compared to the highest priced store.

large). St. Louis, another neighborhood in which store price levels are relatively similar, also offers large savings from item shopping. The largest total savings are attainable in New York where a large amount of scrambled pricing is added to the substantial differences in average price levels.

The formation of accurate perceptions of item differences would require considerable search effort. Fortunately most of the savings can be realized without shopping at every store of the neighborhood. The big jump in savings comes from adding a second store—from 2.8% to 6.4% (see column 2 of Table 5).

Incremental savings from the addition of a third or fourth store are small although the size depends principally on the pricing strategies of the average and high priced stores. The more a high priced store engages in scrambled pricing, the more a shopper can add to his savings by selective purchases at that store. This strategy is most effective if the store offers a limited number of deep price reductions on economically important items. The highest priced New York store follows such a policy. It offers very low prices on several meat items, but its overall meat prices are high.

Another attractive procedure for saving search time is the grouping of items together for purchase decisions. For example, buy all beef products at a single store and all cereal at another. Or put still larger groups together, such as all fresh meat or all dry groceries. The entries in column 4 indicate that very large groupings add minimal savings.[5] Purchases grouped by product category offer larger savings than those available from departmental buying although greater search effort is required. Again a large portion of the savings available could be realized by shopping at only two stores—4.6% of the maximum 5.6%

Two general conclusions appear from these data. (1) Savings can be realized by shopping more than one store in a neighborhood. The possible savings are double or triple those attainable by choosing only the low priced store; the precise amount of savings depends on the complexity of the buying strategy and nature of the store environment. (2) The types of strategies suggested are not going to generate huge savings—probably less than 10%. The shopper must consider whether

[5]Minimal saving should be expected with the present definitions. Only four departments are employed, and 85% of the total weight is given to two departments: dry groceries and fresh meat. Other definitions should produce higher savings.

savings of this magnitude are significant to her. If she considers them significant, she must strike a balance between the savings realizable and the cost of developing an appropriate strategy. She must also determine whether the strategy can be held constant or whether it must be revised frequently.

Stability of Optimal Purchasing Strategies

The more complicated a purchase strategy, the less stable it is over time. Optimal item by item purchasing requires current information every day. The store with the lowest price for ground beef last week is not likely to have that position this week. On the other hand, the store with the lowest overall prices last week very likely is the lowest overall this week. Simple buying strategies retain most of their savings without constant surveillance and revision. But more complex strategies must be continually changed in their detailed purchase instructions.

Table 6 shows the loss in savings if buying strategies are not updated according to current price data. The loss is slight if the housewife is buying everything at the same store. There will be specific dates on which that store may not be the very lowest; but the loss will be small, 11% with the Boca Raton data.

Item by item buying requires extremely close scrutiny in order to realize near-optimal savings. Only about 60% of the savings attainable from shopping four stores would result if the shopper employed the same store/product pairings for each purchase date. This buying strategy must stipulate which products to purchase at which stores, not just "item by item purchasing at four stores." Updating such a strategy requires complete knowledge of all prices for each date. Without revision, the item by item strategy yields only 50% more saving than the strategy of buying all items at a single store.

These data are for only one community and cover only five weeks, but they show the research and monitoring task required for maximum savings. An appealing strategy that might avoid detailed search and yet retain a high degree of savings is to divide items into two groups. Items showing small price differences among stores could be purchased continually at the store with the lowest average price (for those items). The more volatile items could be monitored periodically at the stores most likely to be low in price.

Our purpose is not to select an optimal buying strategy but to indicate the forces that should be considered in such a selection. The starting point is the measurement of potential savings with complete

TABLE 6
INCREMENTAL SAVINGS FROM UPDATED
BUYING STRATEGIES[a]

| Strategy | Percentage Saving | | Percentage Loss from Constant Strategy[d] |
	Updated[b]	Held Constant[c]	
Single Store	3.8	3.4	11
Departmental Buying, 2 Stores	4.8	4.1	15
Product Category Buying, 2 Stores	5.3	4.3	19
Product Category Buying, 3 Stores	5.9	4.5	24
Item Buying, 2 Stores	7.4	4.9	34
Item Buying, 3 Stores	8.0	5.2	35
Item Buying, 4 Stores	8.3	5.1	39

[a]Based on Boca Raton data which were collected on five consecutive weeks, same day of week.

[b]Purchases based on store prices for specific day.

[c]Purchases based on average prices for the five week period.

[d]Column 3 compared to column 2.

information; then, how much the savings will be reduced if sub-optimal strategies are employed. The shopper should first have accurate perceptions concerning the magnitudes of the potential savings. At the second step, if she considers these magnitudes significant, she should perceive the relative price positions of competing stores for individual items and/or overall prices. The potential savings could be economically significant to most families; 5% per year on food purchases would yield almost $100 on the typical food budget.

SAVINGS FROM WHAT, WHEN, AND HOW MUCH

All of the preceding analysis is based upon purchase of the specified market basket at particular points in time. How much can the housewife save by proper timing of her purchases or by minor deviations from the specified items? The data available are limited but show savings that are considerably larger than those available from store selection.

Stockpiling

All stores run specials from time to time on various items, sometimes with price reductions of 20% or more. If the housewife could stock-up at these prices, she would realize savings at least equal to those available from item by item purchasing at several stores. Unlimited stockpiling would yield savings that are almost double those of an item purchase strategy.[6] If purchases are limited to the amount consumed in a four week period, the savings are 5-5½%, still a substantial figure.

Stockpiling decisions cannot avoid predictions. The figures above assume perfect predictive ability, impossible in the real world. Wise buying decisions with respect to stockpiling require an understanding of the market place, of the way prices fluctuate, and of the forces that produce these changes. A memory of past prices is involved, but understanding goes well beyond memory. The more accurately the shopper understands the forces at work in her neighborhood, the closer she can approach the full 5-5½% figure cited.

All products in the market basket cannot be stored for the same length of time. Stockpiling possibilities for fresh produce are almost zero. Canned goods can be kept for months or even years. Stockpiling of goods with stable prices would be unwarranted. Cola, rice, and baby food have been known to remain at the same price for months, suggesting that a stock-up strategy for them may seem inappropriate— but the historical pattern might not hold in the future. The shopper must weigh all these considerations, plus storage facilities, temporary cash shortages, and desired menu variation in her stock-up policy. The gains on a limited number of carefully selected products should warrant the effort.

What Size?

A question somewhat related to stockpiling is what size packages to buy. Price is not the sole criterion. Large sizes are poor purchases,

---

[6]The figures for savings from stockpiling are taken from Robert Lundeen Ziegenhagen, *An Analysis of The Relative Costs of Various Consumer Supermarket Shopping Strategies,* University of Pennsylvania: 1970, unpublished MBA Thesis. The data cover 39 different dates over a period of one year in two sets of four stores each. The data were collected under the supervision of Brown and Oxenfeldt in conjunction with another study.

regardless of price differentials, if the product will spoil before most of it is consumed. If it can be stored satisfactorily and the household uses it in sufficient quantities, large size packages may offer substantial savings.

Large sizes are typically sold at lower prices per unit weight or volume. The smallest sizes are expensive and should be avoided as a general rule. One pound of sugar, a pint of milk, and a two-ounce jar of instant coffee are examples of this rule. The housewife will typically pay at least 50% more (on a unit basis) for these small packages than for the larger sizes.

Table 7 shows the premium paid for small sizes in milk, sugar, and instant coffee. The price increases do not occur in uniform steps, and the price premium patterns are not similar for the three products. Price per pound of sugar is almost identical whether it is purchased in five or ten pound units—the two largest sizes. In fact, specials on sugar almost always occur for the five pound bag, making it lower per pound than the ten pound unit when the special is in effect. In contrast, shoppers pay a premium of almost 10% for the half-gallon container of milk over the gallon container. Substantial increases occur for sugar in

TABLE 7
PREMIUM PAID FOR SMALL SIZES OF
SUGAR, MILK, AND INSTANT COFFEE

| Size[a] | Premium Paid[b] | | |
	Sugar	Milk	Instant Coffee
Smallest	53%	58%	96%
Second Smallest	34	21	5
Average	1	9	2
Large	—	—	—

[a]Sizes are the following:

	Sugar	Milk	Instant Coffee
Smallest	1 lb.	pt.	2 oz.
Second Smallest	2 lb.	qt.	6 oz.
Average	5 lb.	½ gal.	10 oz.
Large	10 lb.	gal.	12 oz.

[b]Price per unit weight or volume of designated size compared to price of large size. All sizes were not available in all stores or communities. Comparisons are based upon average prices of the neighborhood for the specific size/brand for instant coffee and average price regardless of brand for milk and sugar.

the one and two pound sizes. The price per ounce of instant coffee in a two ounce jar is almost double the price in the larger containers. The pattern is further confused by the "cents off" deals which occasionally make the six or ten ounce jars better buys than the largest size.

The precise amount that shoppers can save by avoiding the smallest size packages is uncertain, but it is substantial. Furthermore, this saving can be realized within each store; store to store inspection is not required. The patterns of Table 7 are quite consistent for the various neighborhoods, suggesting that the size/price relationships for specific products may be general for widespread areas.

Brand and Item Selection

Large price differences exist among brands of the same product. These price differences may or may not be accompanied by non-price differences.[7] If they are, the consumer should weigh their significance against the possible savings. She need not buy the lowest priced brand. The highest priced may be her choice, but she should know the price differentials involved.

A typical difference among competing brands for a six-ounce jar of instant coffee or a 29-ounce can of sliced cling peaches is 15-20%. Where a popular national brand is compared to the lowest priced house label, the price difference is usually larger than that. Quality differences, taste preferences, and consumer franchise clearly are pertinent for the purchase decision; but the customer should be aware of the price differentials that exist—again within the same store.

The housewife may make much broader changes in the market basket items than the brand and size. If she simply wants to buy meat and vegetables for the next few days, price differentials among alternatives are astronomical. The permissible range of items differs for each household, but the price range among alternatives is much larger than the 15-20% cited for brand differences.

SUMMARY

The empirical data demonstrate conclusively that differences in food prices are large and complex. Price differences face the shopper at every

---

[7]Non-price factors are also present in all preceding comparisons: services offered, convenience of store lay-out, package design and storability, store accessibility, as well as quality of nonstandardized products. Non-price factors may be somewhat less critical in those cases than where different brands are involved.

turn. Stores differ in price levels and in prices of individual products. Prices change with the passage of time; stores low at one time may be high at another—particularly for individual products. Different brands of the same product are available at different prices, and the same brand is packaged in various sizes—sometimes at drastically different prices per unit.

The perceptive shopper must recognize all these phenomena. She must know which price differences are large and which are small. She must identify the decisions that offer the greatest potential savings, and she must perceive the magnitudes involved for various decisions. Finally, she must recognize the difficulties involved in trying to form accurate perceptions of the various dimensions.

Selection of the lowest priced store offers only modest savings, but that selection can be carried out with limited effort and at modest costs. Depending upon the specific neighborhood conditions, savings on the order of 3% (5% when compared to the highest priced store) are typically attainable without constant monitoring and shopping revisions. Shopping at several stores could increase savings to over 8% but only if specific prices on all items were continually checked. One-stop shopping for most items plus the monitoring of several stores for a few important items would seem the best strategy.

The decisions offering the largest savings—and posing the greatest possible losses if misperceived—refer to package sizes and stock-up policies. Both of these are well within the shopping ability of every housewife. Premiums of over 50% must be paid for small sizes, and the shopper can usually avoid these excessive premiums without going to the very largest package. Stock-up policies for a limited number of items—those most subject to price fluctuations—would yield savings of over 5%.

Brand and item selection represent fundamental departures from the market basket approach, but the savings potential for this type of shift would exceed 25%. Only the constraints imposed by family tastes would establish the limits for savings from these sources.

Part III

How the Perceptual Process Influences Perceptual Accuracy

We believe that an acquaintance with the physical/neurological approach to perception is necessary for the understanding and reduction of economic misperceptions. Chapter VII sketches the general model of the perceptual process as depicted in the psychological literature, and Chapter VIII relates that model to economic phenomena.

Chapter VII represents a fairly sudden change in the level and substance of our discussion, but it provides the foundation for many of our action implications. Readers who skip to Chapter VIII will be able to follow the thread of the discussion and the recommendations advanced for reducing economic misperceptions. They will not, however, have as complete a discussion of how economic misperceptions arise.

Chapter VII

OUTLINES OF A THEORY
OF MISPERCEPTION

This chapter attempts to explain why and how misperceptions arise. We believe it illuminates the subject and suggests plausible hypotheses, but it is only a small first step. Although the discussion is short on answers, it raises questions that should be asked more insistently.

When we say we wish to build a theory of economic misperception, we do not imply that economic misperceptions result from unique processes which are different from those producing other kinds of misperceptions. We expect that the mechanisms by which misperceptions arise are the same in all spheres and anticipate that most of what is said here could be generalized widely, even as we draw heavily upon the general literature of psychology and social psychology. We see the market place as an intensively studied institution which offers great opportunity to learn about representative people in real-life situations, rather than college students in contrived experiments.

PERCEPTION DEFINED

The term "perception" is used rather loosely to apply to a wide range of phenomena. At one extreme, it denotes the message that reaches the brain when a stimulus attended by a sensory organ is transmitted to the brain. These perceptions may be likened to snap-shots, such as fleeting images, momentary sensations of sweetness, heat, or roughness. At the other extreme, perception denotes a highly generalized interpretation of many such sensations both past and present along with logical reasoning. At this extreme, perception is composed of a superset of processes which subsume sensing, interpreting, testing, judging, storing, remembering—and even learning to perceive.

The kinds of perceptions discussed in this book are of the more complex type, e.g., an impression that stores which advertise heavily are generally more expensive than those which do not. We must expect to

99

find many elements underlying such impressions. Some low level perceptions of specific prices and specific instances of advertising are no doubt involved. Some individuals may apply "logical reasoning" to the effect that advertising costs money and stores will try to recapture it in the form of higher prices. Others, just as plausibly, may reason that retailers pay for advertsing from higher sales volume. Still others may add to these elements a general prejudice against advertising—producing a tendency to "blame" advertising for many economic ills.

Perceptions at this extreme closely resemble attitudes. They also may be likened to the generalizations reached on the basis of empirical research. In our illustration, an attitude toward advertising is one of the ingredients contributing to the perception, indicating that some perceptions are even more general than attitudes while simultaneously those attitudes may be partly based upon lower level perceptions. We use the term "perception" to cover this wide range from simple sensation to complex generalizations and impressions. This view of perception follows that of Forgus who defines perception as "the process of information extraction."[1] Perceiving thus involves the processes by which data from the environment are received, transformed into information, and converted into judgments.

Most of the psychological literature on perception is addressed to low level phenomena. We will first sketch the perceptual process at this level, describing it as the formation of "point perceptions." We will then discuss the development of "constructs," the grouping of individual perceptions into classes and some elementary generalizations about them. Finally, we will discuss the formation of attitudes and more particularly attitude change. In these reviews of the process by which different kinds of perceptions are formed, we will mainly try to identify points at which the process may go astray—where distortions might enter and produce a gap between the outer reality and the individual's view of it.

A MODEL OF POINT PERCEPTION

Point perceptions differ from broad perceptions mainly in that they rest very heavily upon the performance of the sensory organs and the mechanisms which transmit impulses from the sensory organs to the

[1] Ronald H. Forgus, *Perception,* (New York, McGraw-Hill, 1966). Chapter I.

brain. Broad perceptions heavily involve the functioning of the brain and the direct sensory content represents a small proportion of the total.

Perception represents a complex of processes which mediate between physical stimuli (objective reality) and the organism's experience of it. The elements that comprise this process include the following:

1. An external reality—sometimes termed an energy flux or a stimulus.

2. A sensory receptor to which the stimulus is presented or by which it is attended.

3. A neural network by which the sensation is transmitted from its point of impact (retina, tastebuds, eardrum) to the central nervous system.

4. A neural system for the encoding of the input.

5. A process by which the input is combined with other prior inputs (learned material).

6. A process for the storage of the input.

7. A process by which sub-cortical reflex behavior is established.

8. A mechanism for the mediation of voluntary responses by higher neural processes (ideation).

In the interest of conciseness, we shall isolate several of these component elements for special attention. Our assumption is that the physical mechanisms for recording stimuli and for sorting and transmitting them are not impaired—though certainly malfunction of these mechanisms is responsible for some misperception. Our main attention revolves around the processes by which the organism attends to some stimuli rather than others, the devices by which sensations are kept from being transmitted to the central nervous system, and the manner in which sensations are related to the stored input of the organism—the role of prior learning.

The Stimulus As An Influence On Accuracy

Opportunities for perceptual distortion vary with the stimuli presented. Phenomena which are unambiguous, unemotional, physically distinct, and familiar are easier to perceive accurately than are their opposites. We would expect larger misperceptions about medical care, cosmetics, psychotherapy, education, travel, patent medicines, and high style clothing than about paper towels, sugar, ball point pens, floor wax, telephone service, and light bulbs.

Most market phenomena are highly complex; the customer usually is concerned with the attributes of the seller, of the product, and even of the company that produces the item. He should take account of the level of technology and the likelihood that it is about to change substantially. He must consider a substantial number of alternative brands and the many different attributes he seeks in the product. Some products are far less complex than others, but very few are truly simple.

The Sensory Receptors

Every organism is supplied with sense receptors to allow it to respond to its environment. In humans these include structures for the detection of light, sound, and heat energies as well as for the detection of pressure and fragrance. Such receptors are complemented by kinesthetic senses which permit transmission of internally produced sensation. Recent evidence demonstrates that human sense receptors allow responsiveness over a large portion of the energy continuum and make very fine discriminations between stimuli along that continuum. This research suggests that a staggering quantity of above-threshold energy fluxes impinge upon our receptors at any time. For example, energy changes of one decibel in sound pressure or two hertz in frequency are sufficient to produce the sensation of different auditory sensations.

Perception involves a selection for transmission among a huge number of possible stimuli. Some of this selection occurs at the receptors. Hermandes-Peon *et al* have demonstrated that certain types of arousal-producing stimuli block stimuli from other sensory organs.[2] More specifically, when an organism is attending to some sound, its ability to sense tastes or to see will be dampened. We expect that similar blocking occurs by raising the thresholds for receptors outside the area of greatest momentary salience. This blocking of competing sensations permits efficient processing of "relevant" stimuli by excluding (or making more difficult) the transmission of less "relevant" stimuli.

[2] R. Hermandes-Peon (Editor), *The Physiological Basis of Mental Activity*, Electroenceph. clin. neurophysiol., 1963, Suppl. 24.

Transmission And Storage

When attended by a sensory receptor, the external stimulus must be encoded. Its form must be changed into the language of the nervous system so that it can be transmitted. Even if this takes place without error and is transmitted over the appropriate neural pathway in the direction of the brain, there is no guarantee that it will enter into focused consciousness. Much stimulation is processed within the spinal cord and brain stem with only slight involvement of the cortex.[3] Unconditioned reflexes are examples of this type of transmission: the sight and smell of food produce salivation by reflex action which is not controlled directly by the higher brain structures. The same holds for conditioned responses such as the movement of the foot to the car brake as one approaches a red light. No ideation or other responses of the higher levels of the central nervous system are required to mediate such conditioned reflexes. The responses are subject to generalization, i.e., a particular response will be made by the organism to a range of stimuli approximating the originally learned stimuli. The traffic light need not be perceived as precisely the same shade of red to evoke the response of the foot's movement to the brake.[4]

Transmitted stimuli which have not been attached to particular responses by previous learning will cause arousal of the central nervous system and subsequent mediating processes which we call "ideation." Faced with a novel stimulus, the organism focuses attention on it, exhibiting what is known as an "orientation reaction." This reaction is characterized by: (1) a low range of sensory thresholds along the relevant sensory modality—the sensory organ and the neural pathways along which it sends its encoded messages, and (2) the blocking of sensation from other modalities. Cortex arousal is also evidenced by higher frequency desynchronized EEG rhythms, skeletal changes which direct the sense organs toward the stimuli (e.g., pricking of ears), arresting of ongoing visceral reactions, a rise in general muscle tone and

---

[3] D. O. Hebb, *A Textbook of Psychology,* Saunders, Philadelphia: 1966, Chapter III.

[4] Conditioned reflexes, in contrast to unconditioned reflexes, can be suppressed by retraining which vitiates the associative links between stimuli and particular responses.

dilation of the blood vessels in the head allowing a greater blood supply to reach the brain.[5]

While the above reactions have been empirically observed, the process which we assume to mediate between the novel stimulus and the organism's response to it is highly speculative. We would suppose that some classificatory process takes place which seeks to match the incoming stimulus with some stored traces of previous stimuli. Some evidence for this supposition is cited by Lynn to the effect that nerve types have been isolated which respond (fire) to stimulus difference or novelty, e.g., a fire when a ninety decibel tone is presented after one hundred presentations of a fifty decibel tone.[6]

This process has an analogy in construct formation wherein an input is placed in a familiar class as a first step in assessing its significance. Previous learning, the ability to discriminate, the number of classes employed, and even the context in which the stimulus occurs, determine what is classified as a "novel" stimulus—one which should be subjected to further scrutiny and perhaps serve as a basis for a new class or a complete new classification system.

We possess ample evidence that organisms store information within their central nervous systems. The process by which this is done and the manner in which past sensations may be altered or lost has not been specified *on the neural level.* Some evidence suggests the existence of memory neurons but the evidence is not conclusive. We know even less about the altering of neural memory traces over time.

The Condition of the Receiver

A variety of intra-psychic and social factors appear to influence the perceptual process. Both the external reality that is attended and the processing of the sensory inputs are affected by the emotional state of the perceiver and by the environment. Such social factors as other people's opinions can direct and alter perception in ways that have been illustrated by the experiments of Bruner and Goodman.[7]

The foregoing examination of the perceptual process—as it relates to "point" perceptions—indicates its major components and suggests

[5] C. E. Lynn, *Attention, Arousal, And The Orientation Reaction,* Oxford: 1966, Page 45.

[6] Lynn, *Op. Cit.*

[7] Bruner and Goodman, *Journal of Abnormal and Social Psychology,* 42, pages 33-44.

mechanisms and junctures at which it may malfunction. The exact nature and interconnection of these components and their functioning have not been empirically determined; much of what we have said is speculative. Nevertheless, we do know that the organism somehow selects for its attention an infinitesimal fraction of the stimuli presented to it. Some stimuli lead to overt behavior without consciousness on the part of the organism (reflexes). More important, organisms relate their perceptions to past knowledge. Some type of classification occurs; indeed some classification is inescapable. Without it, the organism cannot determine whether the stimulus deserves attention and should be passed on to the highest centers of the central nervous system.

A MODEL OF CONSTRUCT FORMATION

Much of psychology deals with the process by which humans form 'constructs," i.e., how they identify classes of objects in the external world. Whereas point perception is a process by which some snap-shot of reality is recorded internally by the organism, a construct is the result of many point perceptions that are processed by the mind. Constructs are invented; they are abstractions which are intended to tie together a body of perceptions.

A construct is composed of items which are functionally equivalent; those stimuli which elicit the same response are subjectively perceived as the same or similar. Whether the perception is accurate depends upon the appropriateness of similar responses to items placed in the same class. Constructs are basically definitions ranging from physical objects such as tables and doors to abstract concepts such as beauty and honor. Items are placed within the same class because the respondent views them as equivalents in some context.

One way or another, humans develop constructs. Most of their knowledge, their actions, and their aspirations involve the processing and manipulation of constructs. Construct formation is complementary to point perception: point perception involves placing items in pre-established classes whereas construct formation involves the establishment of the classes.

Individuals do not usually discriminate among items unless they have been rewarded for making such distinctions in the past. Red lights given from traffic sentinels differ in scores of dimensions that are ignored by auto drivers, largely because they see neither reward for such discrimination nor loss from the failure to discriminate. The novice in a trade employs very gross classification systems for the tools whereas the journeyman uses very precise classes. In "operant conditioning" terms, we would say that discrimination training has occurred with the journeyman.

The formation of constructs is an attempt to balance the economies available from generalization against the possible rewards of specification. The position is well summarized by Carnap in the following quotation,

> Constructs must at first necessarily possess some degree of indefiniteness; there can be no question of any clear delimination of their content. So long as they remain in this condition, we come to an understanding about their meaning by making repeated references to the material of observation from which they appear to have been derived, but upon which, in fact, they have been imposed. Thus, strictly speaking, they are in the nature of conventions—although everything depends on their not being arbitrarily chosen but determined by their having significant relations to the empirical material, relations that we seem to sense before we can clearly recognize and demonstrate them. It is only after more thorough investigation of the field of observation that we are able to formulate its basic scientific concepts with increased precision and consistency over a wide area. Then, indeed, the time may have come to confine them in definitions. The advance of knowledge, however, does not tolerate any rigidity even in definition.[8]

A MODEL FOR THE FORMATION OF ATTITUDES

Point perceptions and constructs are usually rich in empirical content; in contrast, attitudes include personal evaluation, fears, goals, both conscious and unconscious prejudice as well as empirical content. In short, attitudes are highly complex mental phenomena compared with point perception and constructs. Since economic perceptions concerning buyer decisions often contain attitudes or are affected by attitudes, we would expect that an understanding of the formation of attitudes would help explain those perceptions.

The literature on attitudes is mainly addressed to their change rather than to their initial formation. When existing attitudes are

[8]Carnap, 1915, page 117.

explained, it is done on a statistical or "black-box" basis—poor people are more likely to vote democratic than are rich people, certain national groups are more prejudiced against Blacks and Jews than are other national groups, males have higher quantitative aptitudes than females, etc. Persuasive reasons are often induced to account for these relationships, but very little is said to explain the process by which individuals formed these attitudes.

Point perceptions and the constructs built from them may form the basic ingredients for attitudes, but we have found nothing in the psychological literature addressed to this question. It may be that there is no way of knowing when an attitude came into existence. At the time we ask attitudinal questions, we assume that the attitude has existed antecedent to our asking—though the question may bring the attitude into existence.

The senses, the encoding processes, the transmission mechanisms, and the storage and retrieval processes are paramount for point perceptions. The processes of primitive organization by which individuals effect closure, distinguish figure from ground, group similar items, separate dissimilar ones, attach constancy to phenomena which they view inconstantly, and assign depth-distance to items come into play with constructs. Information processing, the formation of judgments, and the review of past decisions play paramount roles in attitude formation. Empirical evidence shows a decreasing degree of consensus among individuals in their interpretations of the same reality as we proceed from point perceptions to constructs and on to attitudes.

The high degree of inconsistency among individuals in their attitudes suggests that the formation of attitudes may be highly unstable and idiosyncratic. The stability of an attitude seems to depend, among other things, upon the strength of the initial forces that produced it, reinforcing and offsetting factors in the interim, and the environmental situation (peculiar to the individual) operative at the time of the research and the time of recent decision making.

Attitudes appear to be vague and without strong commitment until a particular issue is raised. When confronted with a need—and to some extent an opportunity—to take a side, most individuals clarify their positions and strengthen their commitment to these positions. Attitude research always runs the risk of forcing respondents to take positions and express atittudes which heretofore may have been amorphous and ephemeral.[9] The same questions asked at another time might have shown very different attitudes.

Attitudes may also be affected by coinciding events. Logically unrelated activities with similar timing may be linked together in the perceptual process. Correlation and covariance analyses often rely on similarity in timing; general perceptions may employ the same idea without using the formal technique.

In summary, little is known about the formation of attitudes. Most research results have been of a black box type. Most of our attitudes receive some endorsement from outside sources, but the acceptability of various sources is largely idiosyncratic. The great diversity of attitudes, some of which fly in the face of strong evidence, suggests that simple models will be highly unreliable in predictive efficacy and that attitudes on all subjects may be characterized by a high degree of misperception.

The availability of general economic logic is particularly trouble-some to individuals who wish to form accurate perceptions. They can draw upon a plethora of "well established" economic relationships. Unfortunately, there is usually at least one on each side of any question, and the decision maker may choose whichever one happens to best fit his own predispositions.

[9]For a discussion of methodological problems faced in studying latent attitudes see Raymond Bauer and Stephen Greyser, *Advertising in America; The Consumer View,* Boston: 1968.

Chapter VIII

PRINCIPAL SOURCES OF ECONOMICAL MISPERCEPTIONS

The foregoing account of the perceptual process (Chapter VII) permits us to identify the points at which inaccuracy might occur. The chief sources of difficulty can be classified under three factors: the object to be perceived, the perceiver, and the environment in which perception occurs. These factors are most likely to produce misperception through their influence on the allocation of attention and through their influence on the mental processing of information.

The Object To Be Perceived

Proper attention must be paid to external reality if accurate perceptions are to be formed. The observer may not notice the relevant object at all, or he may allocate his attention to irrelevant or trivial characteristics of the object. In judging the amount of goods in a container, for example, he may focus his attention on the size or shape of the container rather than on the number of ounces indicated. In judging the quality of an item, the perceiver may focus his attention on wholly irrelevant or actually misleading clues. He may focus upon a styling feature of an article of clothing, erroneously associating it with the quality of the tailoring.

The characteristics of the external reality—the object to be perceived—will facilitate accurate perceptions in some cases and hamper them in others. The characteristics of the object influence both the allocation of attention and the accuracy of the data processing. Some of the more obvious characteristics are:

1. Saliency
2. Ambiguity
3. Complexity
4. Physical separateness
5. Familiarity
6. Emotionality

These factors may pull in the same direction for some objects and in opposite directions for others. The formation of an opinion about another human being, for example, is filled with complexity and ambiguous information—both contributing to possible misperception. Emotional overtones will also normally be high, adding to the possibility of misperception. The saliency of a personal impression depends upon the relationship envisioned with that person; we would expect high salience to result in more accurate perceptions via increased attention and more careful data processing.

Familiarity is really a relationship between the object and the perceiver. The perceiver's familiarity with the object or similar objects partly determines the probability of misperception. We expect the expert to discriminate between the original and a fine copy; the novice may be fooled by a poor copy. The more distinct the separation between an object and its surroundings, the greater the accuracy of the perception should be. This factor also interacts with the perceiver and depends on the appropriateness of his classification system. The object itself may be displayed or presented in a way that emphasizes or minimizes its physical separateness. Greater attention is required in the latter case than in the former in order to form accurate perceptions.

The Perceiver

The organism to which the stimulus is presented is usually a major contributor to economic misperception. The perceiver—in contrast to the external stimulus—can introduce misperception at any of three stages: (1) the misallocation of attention; (2) the internal communication network, including the sensory organs and the entire neural network for transmission, storage, and retrieval; and (3) the analytical process in which generalizations are formed. As we suggested earlier, these three stages do not operate independently. The perceiver directs his attention in accordance with his concepts of relevance which in turn depend on his information processing plans and prejudices. Individuals also differ in the degree of dependence they place upon different senses. These differences may reflect differential reliabilities for various senses among individuals or different styles regardless of reliability. The point is that a perceiver directs the attention of specific senses to stimuli; attention direction does not call on all senses simultaneously or equally. The internal processing of information in turn depends upon the way in which attention is directed and the reliability with which the internal communication system relays this information.

The amount of attention a perceiver concentrates on a particular object will depend upon his commitment to objectivity, his commitment to prior conclusions, and the importance he attaches to the external object—to name only the more obvious elements. He may be more concerned with justifying past judgments than with developing an accurate assessment. With such a motivation, he may exhibit a low level of attention to the more relevant factors and a high level of attention to certain less relevant factors.

Festinger's stress on dissonance reduction underscores the individual's lack of objectivity.[1] The perceiver does not usually attend items which are inconsistent with his past actions or statements; to do so would increase his anxieties. Similarly, the perceiver will be cognizant of market offerings only if he admits the economic consequences of his selections are important. As long as he can classify the decisions as minor, he can defend his lack of commitment to objectivity and even boast of it.

A slightly different explanation for non-objectivity is related to the complexity of the stimulus/environment. As long as the perceiver does not try to form accurate perceptions, his ego is not damaged by his misperceptions—particularly if he does not know about them. This non-contestant role is particularly attractive for individuals when the perceptual task is complex and difficult. This posture may be further justified if the individual can claim the external object is unimportant to him.

The internal communication system involves the efficiency of the sensing, transmitting, and encoding mechanisms as well as the storage and retrieval capabilities. We are all familiar with the fact that individuals may attempt to recall certain instances by "visualizing" them. These individuals are attempting to reconstruct a certain sensory experience. Other individuals rely more on auditory sensations. Perceptual accuracy should increase when the individual relies on the senses which discriminate best among the items to be compared. The most discriminating sense need not be the same for all individuals. This, of course, is illustrated most dramatically for individuals who have

---

[1]Leon Festinger, *A Theory of Cognitive Dissonance,* Stanford, Calif.: Stanford University Press, 1957.

suffered impairment of one or more senses, e.g., quality control inspection by blind individuals through the sense of touch.

The perceiver's information processing depends upon his general ability in analysis and his specific abilities within a particular substantive field. His *general* ability is reflected in such skills as the ability to perceive relationships, to draw logical conclusions, to apply principles from one discipline to another, and to construct classification systems. The *specific* abilities in analysis relate to his information, classification systems, and power to discriminate *within the narrow field germane to the external stimulus.* A very intelligent but uninformed individual may properly judge the fluency, strength, and manual dexterity of applicants for a position. Without knowledge of the relative weights to give to each of these characteristics or minimum levels requisite for the performance of duties, he is at a loss to choose among the applicants or to determine whether any of the applicants can perform the duties demanded. In much the same way, an individual may form accurate perceptions of irrelevant characteristics by kicking the tires of an automobile and by slamming its doors. It is necessary to identify the relevant characteristics and to assess accurately each option with respect to those characteristics.

The Environment

The environment within which the perceived phenomenon occurs and the environment within which the perceiving organism operates also influence the accuracy of perception. The environmental influence operates chiefly through its effect on the allocation of attention. The many stimuli competing for attention may result in the playing down of relevant factors in favor of the irrelevant factors—particularly if the irrelevant are traumatic or more easily perceived. A loud noise or a sudden movement will divert the subject's attention from an assigned task. The amount of a specific price may not be noted, but the shopper may be aware that it was marked "special."

A pleasant environment mitigates against harsh sanctions or severe penalties. The wife feeds her husband a good meal before telling him of the dent in the car's fender. We leave it to the reader to decide whether this is properly classified as a misperception, but we claim that the environment has a marked influence on the perception that occurs. The opposite phenomena is also common: requests are not made when the petitioned person is in a bad mood. Every child, employee, and lawyer applies this rule.

The perceptual process can be compared to the solution of a regression equation in which the environment is operative in several ways. At the first stage, it supplies a set of independent variables, some of which are rationally chosen for inclusion by the decision-maker and others that are included because of custom or because of their high visibility. These latter variables may also blot out or blur readings of more appropriate variables. At the second stage, environmental factors help determine which variables are called from memory for any particular decision. Finally, at the third stage, the environment adjusts the standard of acceptability—revising the minimum (or maximum) level required of the dependent variable.

SOURCES OF SUPERMARKET MISPERCEPTIONS

The general sources of misperception sketched in the last section are reflected in our supermarket price data. The applicability of our discussion of misperception is seen best in the external reality, i.e., the prices charged by supermarkets for single items or groups of items. The following discussion will be illustrative; an inclusion of all factors would be unnecessarily lengthy.

Complexity Of Reality

It is extremely difficult for even a pricing specialist to determine the price levels of competing supermarkets. The concept of a price index (with or without weights), the kinds of products that should be in the index, the selection of the right sizes and brands, plus the huge number of products within a supermarket make the accurate determination of a store's price level extremely difficult. Such complexity might well result in a high level of misperception despite strong efforts by shoppers to form accurate conclusions about relative prices. Moreover, individuals might despair of forming accurate perceptions and confine their efforts to a few important items.

There is nothing very complicated, however, about the price for a single item such as sugar. Or is there? If we mean the average price of sugar within the neighborhood over the recent past, it is not a very complicated question. If we mean which store has the lowest price for sugar, then the question becomes somewhat more difficult. If store A charges the lowest price one day, store B does the next day, and store C becomes the lowest a week later, the complexity of reality is much greater. If the per pound price relationships for five pounds are not the same as those for ten pounds or two pounds, reality is even more complex. We might also ask how often the price of sugar changes in a particular outlet. This question is somewhat less complicated than the former; although it is not as simple as asking the average price for sugar within the neighborhood.

Our data are generally consistent with the concept that misperception becomes more likely as complexity increases. The more data required to form an accurate inference and the more processing needed—particularly with weights—the higher the rate of misperception. Prices for single items within particular outlets are reasonably well perceived; those for a single product across stores are perceived with less accuracy as are general price levels across stores.

Saliency

The saliency of an external reality denotes the importance that the perceiver attaches to it. The saliency of supermarket prices might be measured by the amount spent for food on a single shopping trip, the amount spent over a longer period of time, or the amount the shopper believed could be saved by judicious shopping. Saliency is further indicated by the relative importance the buyer places on price in contrast to other factors such as quality, cleanliness, or convenience.

The typical consumer believes that competing supermarkets are within 10% of each other in price levels. Our evidence suggests that she does not consider this a significant difference. In her eyes, we are not talking about an item that has high salience; therefore we would expect frequent misperceptions. The data bear this out; indeed the question arises why perceptions are as accurate as they are.

Part of the explanation for the accurate perceptions comes from the fact that some consumers are price conscious. Those for whom price is more salient—who classify themselves as looking harder for low prices or having chosen a store because of its low price level—record more accurate perceptions and raise the overall level of accuracy for all shoppers combined.

We would expect more accurate perceptions for items which have high unit prices than for items with low unit prices. This would apply particularly to large consumer durables and should reach maximum salience in an automobile or a house. Other factors may offset the role of salience for these products. Lack of familiarity and the high emotion often associated with large expenditures would mitigate against accurate price perceptions for high-priced consumer durables. In contrast, the high degree of familiarity and the low emotional content should add to the accuracy of price perceptions for food.

The effect of salience introduces an interesting twist in the formation of perceptions. Most housewives select certain products as prototypes for judging a store's relative price level. Sometimes only a single item is chosen, and the list rarely exceeds five or six items. Her perceptions of stores' prices for these items will usually be fairly accurate. But the reliability of her list as an indicator for the entire store is usually low, and therefore she often misperceives the store's relative price level. This same phenomenon has been observed in a current research project on employee perception. Employees tend to evaluate an employer's entire fringe benefit program from a single fringe offering such as pensions or health and welfare insurance.[2]

Perceiver Characteristics

The storage/retrieval capability of the perceiver, her commitment or noncommitment to objectivity, and her use of classification systems all influence the accuracy of her perceptions. Low storage/retrieval capacity contributes uniformly to misperception, but the effects of the others are unclear.

The accurate calculation of store price levels (based on a limited market basket) involves a complex computer program.[3] The collection of the basic data requires specific instructions and schedules which are several pages long. These tasks are well beyond the unaided storage/retrieval capabilities of the typical human. Any attempt at weights even with a small number of items, quickly taxes human processing limits. Perception of prices for specific individual items, including a short time span, are well within the shopper's capability. The accuracy of price perception for stated single products depends on other factors such as salience.

---

[2]This project is currently being conducted by F. E. Brown and Wayne Howard of the University of Pennsylvania.

[3]Our attempt to use desk calculators proved highly unreliable, despite elaborate precautions.

A commitment to objectivity normally leads to more accurate perception, although complications usually arise in efforts to execute an objective approach. Formal definitions of methodology should not be expected from food shoppers, but what does constitute "objectivity"? An attempt to "know" prices, shopping the ads, and similar activities are probably the best indicators we have. However, these activities may make the shopper well-informed about the obvious factors—or worse yet, about the factors that the store owner wants to impress on her. Our data suggest that commitment to objectivity (as we have measured it) makes a very small contribution to accurate perceptions, and we suspect it is because the task is so difficult. For items with greater salience and less complexity, we would expect attempts at objectivity to yield more accurate perceptions.

We believe an individual's classification system is of paramount significance in determining the accuracy of her perceptions. Most women establish classification systems based on a combination of logic and empirical data. The more common characteristics employed in classifying stores are size, amount of advertising, trading stamp status, and independent versus chain. The shopper places individual stores in particular categories based on one or more of the characteristics, concluding that general price levels for stores within a given category are similar unless the evidence to the contrary is very strong.

Our earlier discussion of store cues illustrates that classification systems may lead to misperceptions in some instances and accurate perceptions in others. If a housewife employs very refined bases of cross-classification, including many operating characteristics and at least some sample price data, she should form accurate perceptions more consistently. We believe the consumer invites misperception and encourages the store to stress externals if she bases her decisions on these externals. A store may be able to generate a lower price image by eliminating certain services or activities even though it does not cut overall prices. In such a situation, we should not be surprised to find shifts in price perception without any change in price level.

Environmental Characteristics

The environment contributes heavily to misperception of food prices. Each food store attempts to direct the shopper's attention to its low prices. In-store promotions, newspaper ads, and throw-aways all tell of particular "specials" and try to convey the impression that "specials" are almost general.

Other environmental features divert the shopper's attention from the price dimension. The quality of the food, the comfortable and convenient store lay-out, and the store personnel call for their share of the shopper's limited attention. The allocation of attention to non-price features reduces the awareness of price, but the effect on the *accuracy* of price perceptions is conjectural. Supposed relationships between non-price features and price may take over. If the relationship applies to this specific instance, no misperception results. Even if it does not apply to this instance, systematic misperception would result only if the actual relationship is the reverse of the one assumed.

Environmental factors may play a big role in changing the standards the shopper employs to evaluate stores. A congenial atmosphere could make high prices more acceptable. It is a short step to the next stage of classifying the store as lower in prices than reality warrants. At that stage the environment becomes a source of misperception.

Finally, the general atmosphere of food shopping tends to reduce the commitment to objectivity. Many housewives believe the less time spent on the task, the better. Impulse purchases are encouraged, both by the store and the shopper's visualization of later enjoyable consumption. If a price is not marked, it seems petty to inquire. All of these pressures reduce objectivity and probably contribute to misperceptions.

The big sources of environmental distortion seem to be two, both having to do with the direction of attention. (1) Attention is directed by the store toward a limited number of items—items the shopper is led to perceive as low in price. The consumer is told (implicitly or explicitly) that the price has been reduced and is lower than competitors' prices for similar items. This step reduces the perceived risk associated with price levels and permits the second step. (2) Attention is directed toward non-price elements. If the shopper is convinced that the risk associated with price is minimal, she feels justified in using quality, convenience, display, and service as the bases for purchase decisions. The low salience given to price then leads to greater price misperception.

SUMMARY

Psychological literature is rich in discussion of the physical basis of point perceptions—those for which the sensory contribution is large. The evidence for perceptions dealing with ideation and attitudes is sparse. Unfortunately economic misperceptions principally involve these phenomena, with the result that for them explanations in terms of human perceptual apparatus are largely speculative.

We believe attitudinal misperceptions arise most often because of misallocated attention and misdirected mental processing of received data. Misdirected processing may include improper classification systems, failure to weight observations, poor retrieval systems—in general, an inability to cope with a large amount of data.

The object to be perceived, the perceiver, and the environment all contribute to possible misperception. The host of factors calling for attention must be carefully screened for relevance if the consumer is to form accurate perceptions. Multiple goals, the relative importance of conflicting goals, the consistency of signals, and emotional involvement are among the many factors that determine whether attention will be allocated according to the consumer's needs.

Part IV

Action Implications

The empirical results of Part II show the importance of economic misperceptions in food shopping, and Part III suggests explanations for these misperceptions. Part IV extends the discussion to economic misperceptions in general and discusses the action implications of the findings for businesses, consumers, public officials, and academic researchers.

Chapter IX

CONCLUSIONS AND IMPLICATIONS

Misperceptions prevail in the economic sphere as in every other sphere of life. The significance of such misperceptions can be found in the answers of several questions. How large are economic misperceptions? Are they uniformly distributed across all phases of economic life? What are the costs of these misperceptions? Are these costs borne equally by all segments of our society? What actions, public or private, could reduce the incidence and costs of misperceptions? Who, if anyone, should be expected to take steps to reduce misperceptions?

Economic analysis has typically moved in either of two diverse directions: the study of reality or the study of image. These two directions result in preoccupation with either changing the offerings—with inadequate attention given to the communication process—or with manipulation of the communication process for image-making purposes with little concern for the nature of reality. Our empirical research has embraced both reality and perception with concentration on the comparison of the two. Only through such comparisons can meaningful answers be given to the questions raised in the first paragraph.

THE IMPORTANCE OF ECONOMIC MISPERCEPTION

The importance of economic misperceptions is best stated in three general conclusions.

1. Misperceptions are a general phenomenon shared by all individuals and common to all phases of economic life.

2. The incidence of misperception is not uniform. Individuals differ in perceptual accuracy, and the accuracy of perception varies according to the economic phenomenon considered.

3. Some economic misperceptions are substantial in magnitude.

Misperceptions Are General

Economic misperception is pervasive. It occurs in a wide variety of activities, and it is shared by the various participants of any specific activity. Finally, misperception strikes at all social classes.

The supermarket data demonstrate the pervasiveness of misperceptions in various food purchase decisions. The existence of misperceptions in other purchase situations is part of the challenge facing every marketing manager. Its extension to other areas such as employee perceptions is logically sound and consistent with preliminary data.

All participants in purchase transactions share in misperceptions. Both buyers and sellers misperceive reality. Our interviews suggest that no level on the selling side is immune from misperception. Executives at corporate headquarters, store managers, and store clerks are alike in their inability to rank the relative prices of competing stores. In other realms, we suspect that employers suffer from misperception even as employees; borrowers, even as lenders; and educators, even as students.

Misperception is common to all social classes. Attempts to identify the social classes most prone to misperception revealed very little consistency. Motivation, specific experience, and general abilities all contribute to the formation of more accurate perceptions; but these factors typically pull in different directions within the same social class. We expect that the same conclusion—misperception occurs within all social classes—will be found in economic activities other than food purchases.

Misperceptions Are Not Uniformly Distributed

Both the incidence of misperception and the loss produced by it are unevenly distributed. We must study the particular activity and locality before we can estimate the impact of any specific misperception.

Our data show highly accurate perceptions in some communities or for some decisions and woefully inaccurate perceptions in others. Large differences also exist among individual shoppers: almost perfect rankings by a few persons to worse than random rankings by others.

Unfortunately, the distribution of misperception over social classes suggests that those least able to pay the penalty of misperception are most likely to be beset by it. Both low income and low education are associated with larger misperceptions. Fortunately the relationship is weak, but the social consequences still may be severe.

Where Is Buyer Misperception Most Likely?

The non-uniform distribution of buyer misperception is partially explained by the nature of the product purchased. Products for which price misperceptions are most likely are intangibles, items with high emotional overtones, and infrequently purchased items. Another situation that often gives rise to misperception is the multiple item purchase.

The feed-back mechanism, familiarity with alternatives, and the existence of well-established standards are all related to the ease with which accurate perceptions are formed. All three factors are low in the case of intangibles and emotionally charged items. The consumer has little knowledge of appropriate standards for judging professional services and no good way of comparing alternative offerings before the fact. Even after the fact, he has great difficulty in evaluating the wisdom of his action. The desire for the miraculous, typical in health and beauty aids, invites non-objectivity and high emotional involvement. These factors would contribute to inaccuracy even without the reinforcing promotional activity of sellers and manufacturers.

Infrequently purchased consumer durables and multiple item purchases add complexity to the perceptual problem. Lack of direct comparability among alternatives contributes to the difficulty as does the use of out-dated information. Any routine decision runs this risk, but the risk is magnified with increases in the time interval since the last search.

The salience of particular purchase decisions should mitigate against costly misperceptions—*should* but not necessarily *will*. A house purchase represents a large dollar expenditure, but it is also an area where most consumers have little experience. Extended search activity, rational appraisal and comparison, plus the solicitation of expert guidance are ways of avoiding gross misperception. Most home buyers employ at least a minimum of these safeguards in order to avoid costly mistakes. This high salience is fortunate because almost every other aspect of the home purchase invites misperception.

Other Economic Spheres Where Misperception Is Likely

The same factors—emotional involvement, lack of familiarity, complexity of the phenomena, and nonstandardized offerings—are common in other economic spheres where misperceptions are most likely to be significant. The selection of a career is characterized by all of these factors. Fortunately salience is also high. But salience is not sufficient to insure perceptual accuracy; guidance is needed in structuring appropriate decision criteria.

In the same way, decisions with respect to place of employment, type of education, and place of education have large potentials for misperception. We suspect that the complexity of these decisions and the lack of familiarity frequently produce an emotional approach and gross misperceptions.

Investment decisions by the non-professional investor may also exhibit a high level of misperception. The professional investor, even when aided by sophisticated models and high speed computers, finds the balancing of multiple investment objectives, the choice of appropriate investment types, and the choice of specific vehicles within investment types a difficult perceptual task. How much more difficult it must be for the non-professional.

Magnitude and Cost Of Economic Misperception

Price reality differences in food shopping vary from 4% to over 25%, depending on the decision considered and the specific environment. Some consumers show practically no awareness of these differences, and a few even reverse the reality ratings—with the result that the magnitude of misperception often exceeds 10% on price alone.

Quality and service, being more complex and less objective than price, are more subject to misperception. This is true for food and even more likely for technically complex products. The situation would be even worse for long range decisions involving education and occupation. We would like to think that the importance of these decisions would mitigate against large misperceptions; unfortunately, this does not appear to be the case.

Competition And A "Rational Minority"

The significance of economic misperceptions would be reduced if competition produced an equalization of values. The information we have about the relative merits of product offerings shows that such is not the case. Agencies that specialize in the rating of product quality find very substantial differences in values offered by different producers—and these usually cannot be attributed to variations in the desires of the market segments to which the producers are trying to appeal.

A "rational minority" has been said to exercise a policing influence on the market. According to this view, buyers who are accurate perceivers patronize the vendor who offers the best values. Since all of them behave in the same manner, their patronage constitutes a major gain to the vendor they patronize. Conversely, other sellers are penalized because they do not receive any of this patronage. According to the argument, the market disciplines sellers who warrant punishment and rewards the virtuous even if most buyers misperceive.

Two central factors are ignored in this position. First, the crucial tenet of market segmentation is that substantial differences exist among buyers' goals and values. Different market segments are best satisfied by different combinations of goods and services. The rational minority (those who perceive accurately) would not all belong to the same market segment and would not patronize the same vendors. Second, the number of rational buyers is critical. If the rational minority represents only 10% of the total market, it will not count for more than any other 10% who behave in some other manner—a manner based on misperceptions.

In summary, we find economic misperceptions to be both pervasive and important. Measurements of their magnitudes (beyond food prices) await further research, but the forces of competition will not alleviate the inaccuracies and inequities.

IMPLICATIONS: PUBLIC POLICIES

Public agencies have three weapons for reducing the economic losses produced by misperception:

1. Labeling requirements and/or supplementary information from the seller.

2. Government publications.

3. Control over the nature of the offerings.

The first two deal with the problem by providing additional information; the third attempts to control reality.

The least controversial approach concerns the information given by the seller to the buyer. Food and drug labeling, truth in lending,

prospectus requirements by the SEC, and unit pricing are all illustra-
tions of this approach. In order to be effective, the information
provided must be understandable and relevant to the decision-maker;
and he must use it intelligently. Intelligent use means that the consumer
must compare alternatives, using whatever information is available. This
comparison cannot be made without a certain amount of search effort
on the part of the consumer. His effort can be facilitiated by public
agencies in the information requirements they place upon manufacturers and middlemen. Unfortunately, this information is used most
by those least in need of it, i.e., the more affluent and better educated
who can most easily help themselves and who can best bear the
financial cost of wrong decisions.

Certain types of publicity releases by public agencies could be
helpful. Government test results should be published and brands should
be named. Identification of appropriate product characteristics for
different uses would aid many decision-makers. Various quasi-public
groups provide some of this information at present. However, the
information is not widely dispersed, samples are sometimes small and
unrepresentative, and the weighting schemes used for product characteristics may not be appropriate for all market segments.

Information releases should contribute to a reduction in
economic misperceptions, but their immediate effects will probably be
minimal. The principal beneficiaries in the short run will be those
individuals who are currently most conscious of the problem. Our
research indicates that these are the individuals who are the most
accurate perceivers already. Those with the most to gain would be the
hardest to reach.

Legislative action which stipulates acceptable product characteristics or sellers' modes of operation is more likely if health or safety
would be endangered by inferior offerings. Drugs, food, fabrics, and
construction are all illlustrations of this approach. Consumers are
protected from their own misperceptions. Regulatory authorities are
not confident that information and inspection necessarily lead to
accurate perceptions and wise purchase decisions. They, therefore,
remove from the market place those offerings which would have the
most serious consequences if the consumer failed to perceive their true
nature.

"Serious consequences" should not be limited to the usual
definition of health and safety. The groups that are most deprived

should be given extra help and protection. Typically these will be the groups with low current incomes and a low probability of increasing their earning power. Any measures that protect these segments from inferior offerings and their own misperceptions should receive high priority.

Control of offerings is more pressing for necessities than for luxuries. This is an alternative approach to the deprivation dimension. Need is a joint function of the item and the purchaser. Both should be considered. High prices in the ghetto are a more serious problem than high prices in the suburbs. Similarly, the price and quality of mass transportation facilities are of greater concern than the price and quality of auto rentals.

Another dimension relevant in establishing priorities for legislative action is the existing level of offerings. If all alternatives available are of low acceptability, intervention is more justified than if a few superior alternatives are also present. A high priced food store is much more of a problem if it has no competitors than if two or three low priced stores are in the same neighborhood.

Consumer apathy in the face of unacceptable reality offerings is a type of misperception. It is not a misperception with respect to knowledge of existing offerings but a misperception with respect to potential offerings. This is where consumer protection advocates can be most effective; they can alert the consumer not only to what is but also to what could be. Information and publicity in these cases has recently been most effective in bringing about a two-fold correction of existing ills: partially through moral suasion directed to the business community and partially through the introduction of new legislation.

We must be careful in the public policy area. Our proposals should rest on well documented evidence and reflect value scales that are shared by a broad cross-section. If the preceding recommendations violate these criteria, they should also be rejected. Well documented empirical relationships are a better basis for action than plausible theories, regardless of who presents the theories.

IMPLICATIONS: WHAT CAN THE BUYER DO ABOUT MISPERCEPTIONS?

The buyer can cope with the misperception problem in only two ways: conscious efforts to minimize his probability of misperceiving and support of governmental action that will reduce the cost of misperception when it occurs. The first requires a structuring of his decision-making process, one approach being the general model used in this report. The second calls for general grass roots support of legislative attempts to enforce higher performance standards for selected products. Information and education programs do not *per se* reduce the costs of misperception; they contribute (if effective) to the reduction of misperception itself. Indirectly, and in the long run, such programs may exercise a disciplinary constraint on the actual market offerings.

The buyer's best procedure in the short run is to structure his decisions more precisely. Our suggestions focus on two questions.

1. Which product characteristics are most critical? The buyer must concentrate his attention on these and not be misled by trivial features.

2. Do alternative sources differ significantly with respect to these characteristics—*significantly* as defined by the user? If all alternatives are approximately equal, the buyer should give his attention to other decisions.

For multiple item purchases, the buyer should stress the *items* that are most critical and in which alternatives are most dissimilar.

The mere act of structuring the purchase decision has positive benefits. The buyer will no longer drift into a decision; he now must defend (at least to himself) the basis for his selection. We recommend the conscious consideration of four sub-decisions: what, where, when, and how much. This approach automatically guides the buyer to those aspects of the purchase that offer the greatest payoffs. We have found the time element offers potentially large savings (or losses) for food shopping, but other sub-decisions may be more critical for other products.

The buyer must resist the urge to base his decision on easily determined cues. Appearance and "feel" are often poor indicators of durability. The size of the company may be even worse, and the price may be worst of all. In a somewhat similar phenomenon, we have found that quality and service offerings are unreliable cues for the price levels of supermarkets. The existence of an average relationship between the relevant characteristic and some cue is just not a sufficient basis for reaching important decisions; information about the dimension itself must be ascertained.

IMPLICATIONS: WHAT CAN THE SELLER DO ABOUT MISPERCEPTIONS?

The seller can attempt to correct existing misperceptions, or he can accommodate to them. Let us consider two different cases: the first where the misperception works to the disadvantage of the seller and the second where it works to his advantage.

A seller who carries high quality merchandise but is thought to offer mediocre quality has a serious problem. He can either attempt to correct the misperception through publicity and information, or he can change his style of operation. The best procedure for him depends upon the reason for the misperception. If it is based upon strong preconceptions or a well-documented historical past, it may be a long and perhaps losing battle to try to change those perceptions. He may be well advised to change his mode of operation to one that conforms more closely to consumers' preconceptions. This approach calls for an operation that gives a series of signals that are internally consistent and also consistent with reality. He may either adopt new policies that are more consistent with high quality, e.g., modern fixtures, extra services, and perhaps even higher prices; or lower his quality level, accepting the image the public has given him. In either case, he is accommodating to existing misperceptions.

What of the seller who benefits from existing consumer misperceptions? His prices are unusually high, but his customers think they are about average. It is not realistic to expect him to try to correct these misperceptions; indeed most businessmen do all they can to create favorable images that redound to their benefit. At the very least, businessmen must be expected to do all they can to protect themselves against competitors' attempts to secure unwarranted advantages.

Whether the seller accommodates to misperceptions or attempts to correct them the starting point for his actions should be an understanding of the cause. He should know that overall image is determined by many different variables and that consistency among these variables produces a more stable image. He should recognize that many consumers rely heavily on a few easily observed cues as guides for an overall appraisal of an enterprise. Each seller must relate these patterns to his own market segment; there is no universally "best" image for all market segments. He must determine the most important factors for his market; only then can he select policies that are likely to produce favorable perceptions and results.

A strategy that attempts to correct existing misperceptions seems advisable under only two situations: the seller is locked into his current mode of operations, or the misperceptions are not firmly established. A much more likely strategy would be the use of existing misperceptions for the store's advantage. Under this strategy, the store would adopt widely accepted cues without changing the basic offerings to customers. Finally, the store could adopt a more neutral strategy by accommodating to existing folklore.

We trust that in the long run greater publicity will be given to the common causes of misperceptions, that the complexity of relationships will be more widely understood, and that the multiplicity of factors will be recognized. Greater awareness of the extent of misperceptions and their sources should lead to reduction of their magnitudes. The more widespread this awareness among public officials and consumers, the more difficult it will be for the individual seller to create misperceptions for his benefit.

We do not expect that misperceptions will decrease greatly over the next few years. Sellers will continue to play games, attempting to convince the consumer by cues, modes of operation, and specific offerings that their outlets are the preferable sources of supply. Consumers, on the other hand, will play guessing games with the seller attempting to reach broad generalizations about complex phenomena from a limited amount of data. We trust that each will be more conscious of the game the other is playing. We earnestly request that public officials help terminate the game.

AREAS FOR FURTHER RESEARCH

We see misperceptions as pervasive throughout our economy. The empirical portion of this report involved extensive field work but touched only a small aspect of a particular buyer decision: the price dimension of consumer food purchases. Much more work is needed in order to test some of the hypotheses concerning the factors that are most likely to lead to buyer misperception.

Dimensions other than price and the combination of several dimensions into a total buying decision have been virtually untouched at the empirical level. Once more, as was true in the case of price, definitions and measurement techniques will be required for these other dimensions on both the reality level and the perception level. Alternative definitions of reality should be investigated; this may be particularly true with respect to the definition of quality for complex products.

We suspect that the cost of misperception may be even greater in the areas of education and employment than in food purchasing. Huge commitments of time and financial resources are made in these areas both by the individual and society as a whole. A choice is made among alternatives in each case, presumably based upon estimates of the financial and non-financial rewards that will be realized. The measurement problem will be difficult in studies of these areas, but some first approximation of the magnitude of misperception and cues associated with those misperceptions will aid both diagnosis and prescription.

Finally, better measures of the costs of misperception should be derived, costs both to the individual and to society. The basic approach employed in this project stopped at expressed price perception, assuming that purchase behavior is related to that perception. We believe this to be an acceptable procedure as a first approximation, but the true cost of misperception must refer to actual purchase behavior. The weighted function of several dimensions will require utility transformations. On the theoretical level, these pose no difficulty. But if we wish to know the economic significance of misperception, we must get the real counterpart of that utility.

The answers and speculations presented in this report are but a small first step toward the development of a perceptual economics. We believe that further research focusing on this area will contribute toward increased individual and social welfare. The mines of this new subject are deep and virtually untouched; we encourage others to join in the exploration.

LIST OF APPENDICES

Appendix A.

SHOPPER SAMPLE

The total sample consisted of 1063 consumer-shoppers from the five neighborhoods, ranging from 154 in Greensboro to 275 in Havertown.

TABLE A-1
SOCIO-ECONOMIC CHARACTERISTICS OF SAMPLE,
BY COMMUNITY

	Community				
Characteristic	Greensboro	Havertown	New York	St. Louis	San Francisco
Income (Household)					
Median	$6,200	$6,900	$5,100	$6,200	$6,500
% over $10,000	9%	7%	8%	6%	4%
% under $4,000	13%	7%	28%	13%	14%
Age (Shopper)					
Median	37	46	42	49	46
% over 65	6%	7%	12%	18%	9%
% under 25	18%	2%	6%	8%	3%
Education (Shopper)					
Median (Years)	15	12	12	12	12
% College Graduates	44%	12%	28%	14%	8%
Size of Household					
Median	2	4	3	3	3
% over 4	8%	29%	24%	29%	19%
Working Status (Shopper)					
% Employed	55%	26%	48%	29%	38%
Sex (Shopper)					
% Female	85%	94%	89%	91%	86%
Children in Household					
% Yes	40%	73%	56%	66%	50%
Marital Status (Shopper)					
% Married	73%	95%	72%	87%	85%
Number of Completed Interviews	154	275	187	264	183

These figures include only completed questionnaires. There were 40 incomplete questionnaires from the five neighborhoods; these were not included in the present report. Another 50 persons regularly shopped for food beyond their immediate neighborhoods and were also excluded from this study.

Selected socio-economic data for the shoppers of each area are presented in Table A-1. These figures refer only to the individuals within the sample. Actual neighborhood figures may be somewhat different since socio-economic data are missing for approximately 15% of the universe.

Appendix B.

QUESTIONNAIRE SCHEDULE AND INTERVIEWER INSTRUCTIONS

Perceptions, shopping attitudes and behavior, socio-economic data, and related information were collected by personal interview. The interview schedule and interviewer instructions used in Havertown are presented in this Appendix. Those used in other areas were modified as required by local conditions, principally a matter of changing store names.

The interview typically required 30-45 minutes. The most difficult portions involved the perceptual questions. Respondents often gave an initial "I don't know"—seemingly to avoid the possibility of giving an incorrect answer. Probing and the establishment of rapport were required in many instances before the respondent voiced her perception of the various market phenomena. A half day of training and the detailed instruction sheet were well worth the effort. Interviewers were thus sufficiently aware of the potential problem areas and the crucial nature of certain questions.

Flash cards were used for several portions of the interview. Age and income were coded with letters so that the respondent identified her classification by a letter response rather than a dollar or year figure. The names of supermarkets and small neighborhood stores were on separate cards so the respondent could keep them clearly in mind as she discussed the "neighborhood" stores.

Newspaper articles announcing the study appeared in the Greensboro and Havertown papers. These articles gave the interviewers added confidence and interest, and they probably helped gain cooperation.

The record of attempts made on page 1 of the questionnaire permitted efficient scheduling of call-backs. The need for an evening or week-end call could be indicated along with any other helpful information concerning employment hours or vacations. The final response rate for the total study was just under 85%.

How do you do. My name is _____.

I am part of a team that is making a study of food shopping in this area for several college professors at Penn and Columbia. I'd like to ask you some questions about your food shopping and your opinions of food stores.

1. Do you do most of the food shopping for this family? Yes____ No ____

    If yes, proceed with interview.

    If no, who does most of the shopping?

    Could I please speak with her (him)? Yes____ No____

    If yes, proceed to interview.

    If no, when would be the best time to talk to her (him)?_____

2. Do you do most of your food shopping in this area? Yes____ No____

    (Area extends from Manoa Shopping Center to the Food Fair at Township Line and Earlington Road and from the A&P on Westchester Pike to the Acme at Eagle and Darby Roads).

    If yes, make interview.

    If no, where do you do most of your food shopping?_____

    Why do you shop there? _____

    _____

    _____. Terminate interview.

Address: _____

		Date	Time	Result
Call	1:			
	2.			
	3.			
	4.			
	5.			
	6.			

1. How much enjoyment do you receive from food shopping? A lot (1) _____, Some but not a lot (2)_____, Very little (3) _____.

2. How much thought and effort do you devote to your food shopping? A lot (1)_____, Some but not a lot (2)_____, Very little (3) _____.

3. How much satisfaction do you receive in doing a good job as a food shopper? A lot (1)_____, Some but not a lot (2)_____, Very little (3)_____.

4. Do you think you do a better job in shopping for food than most shoppers in this area? Better (1)_____, About the same (2)_____, Not as good (3)___.

5. Do you think you look harder for low prices than most shoppers in this area? Harder (1)_____, About same (2)_____, Not as hard (3) _____.

6. How often do you make a shopping list before you go on a major shopping trip? Usually (1)_____, Sometimes (2) _____, Hardly ever (3) _____. If yes or sometimes, do you try to prepare a complete shopping list or only note those items you are afraid you might forget? Complete (1) _____, Items I'm afraid I might forget (2) _____.

7. Would you describe yourself as a careful reader of food advertisements? Yes (1)_____, No (2) _____.

8. How often do you compare the prices advertised by the different stores? Usually (1) _____, Sometimes (2) _____, Hardly ever (3) _____.

9. How many times a week do you make a large food purchase? _____ a week. About how many times a week do you make additional food purchases? _____ a week.

10. Do you believe that most housewives are good food shoppers? Yes (1) _____, No (2) _____.

11. **Is there a particular day** on which you usually do your main food shopping?
    Yes (1) _____, No (2) _____.
    If yes, what day _____.
    About when during the day do you do your main food shopping?

12. Do you usually do your main food shopping at the same store? Yes (1)_____,
    No (2) _____.
    If yes, at what store? (Enter at A)
    Why do you shop at that store rather than others? (Check appropriate
    reasons at A)
    If no, at what two stores do you shop most often? (Enter most often store
    at A and second at B).
    Let's consider each one separately. Why do you shop at _____?
    (Check under A). Why do you shop at _____? (Check under B).

A. _____ Reasons: Friendliness (1) _____, Price (2)____,
   Store No. 1
   Good Values (3) _____, Overall Quality (4) _____, Convenience(5)_____,
   Meats (6) _____, Produce (7) _____, Assortment (8) _____, Service (9)____,
   Other (10) _____

   _____

B. _____ Reasons: Friendliness (1)_____, Price (2)____,
   Store No. 2
   Good Values (3) _____, Overall Quality (4) _____, Convenience (5) _____,
   Meats (6) _____, Produce (7) _____, Assortment (8) _____. Service (9)____,
   Other (10) _____

   _____

13. At what store do you buy most of your fresh meat? _____.
    Why do you buy your meat there? (Check appropriate reasons).
    Friendliness (1)_____, Price (2)_____, Good Values (3)_____,
    Quality (4)_____, Convenience (5)_____, Assortment (6)_____.
    Service (7)_____, Buy Everything There (8)_____, Other (9)_____

    _____

14. At what store do you buy most of your fresh produce? _____
    Why do you buy your produce there? (Check appropriate reasons).
    Friendliness (1)_____, Price (2)_____, Good Values (3)_____,
    Quality (4)_____, Convenience (5)_____, Assortment (6)_____,
    Service (7)_____, Buy Everything There (8)_____, Other (9)_____

15. If you suddenly ran out of something (like milk, bread, or coffee) at what store would you ordinarily get it? First suppose it was during regular store hours?_____. Suppose it happened during the evening or Sunday, where would you go? _____.

16. Here is a list of supermarkets in the area. Are there any of these stores you would not patronize for reasons other than price - things like poor quality, bad service, not clean, limited selection, too crowded, and factors like that? Yes (1)_____, No (2)_____.
    If yes, which stores? (Enter under store).
    Why would you exclude each one? (Enter under reason).
    Store:_____ Reason: _____
    Store:_____ Reason: _____

17. Considering only goods of equal quality, which one of these stores has the lowest overall prices?_____. The next lowest? _____
    Which one has the highest overall prices - for goods of equal quality?
    _____. The next highest? _____

18. How much did you spend for your last major food order? _____. How much difference do you think there would have been in the total cost for that order between the highest store and the lowest priced store (name the two stores selected by the respondent) ? _____.

19. How much did you spend for fresh meat in that order?_____. How much for fresh produce?_____. Which of the stores do you think would have been the most expensive for fresh meat? _____. the least expensive?_____
    How much difference do you think there would have been between these two stores for the meat you purchased? _____

    Which large store in the area do you think would have been the most expensive for the fresh produce? _____. the least expensive? _____
    How much difference do you think there would have been between these two stores for the produce you purchased? _____.

20. 1. Which of the items on this list are most important in <u>your</u> <u>food</u> <u>store</u> buying? (Enter under item in column 1. After items are entered, take each item and ask across).

    2. What brand and size do you buy most often?

    3. At what store?

    4. What has been its usual price at that store during the past 2 or 3 weeks - <u>ignoring</u> <u>specials</u>?

    5. What is the lowest price at which that store has offered the item in the past 2 or 3 weeks?

    6. The highest price?

    7. a. How frequently does the price of this item change at that store? (Record 1 - for several times a month, 2- about once a month, 3- every few months, 4- very rarely).

       b. Do you think its price at that store has changed during the past three weeks? If yes, how many times? (Record 0, 1-2, or 2+).

       c. When the price is changed, by how many cents is it usually changed?

    8. Considering the major supermarkets, how much difference do you think there would be between the highest priced store and the lowest priced store on a typical non-special day?

    9. Do you think your store is (1) <u>higher than others</u>, (2) <u>about the same</u>, or (3) <u>lower than others</u> for this item?

			Prices		
(1) Item	(2) Brand and Size	(3) Store	(4) Usual	(5) Lowest	(6) Highest
1.					
2.					
3.					
4.					
5.					

(7) Price Changes				(8) Difference Among Stores	(9) Your Store's Prices Compared to Others
Item	(a) Long Period	(b) 3 Weeks	(c) Amount		
1.					
2.					
3.					
4.					
5.					

21. How would you classify the different stores in quality of fresh meat.- <u>ignoring</u> <u>the question</u> of <u>price</u>? Use the categories (1) above average, (2) average, or (3) below average. (Enter number in column 21).

22. How would you rate the quality of fresh produce at each store - again ignoring the question of price? (Enter number in column 22).

	(21) Meat Quality	(22) Produce Quality		(21) Meat Quality	(22) Produce Quality
Acme (Eagle)	_____	_____	Food Fair	_____	_____
Acme (W.C.P.)	_____	_____	Martel	_____	_____
A & P	_____	_____	Penn Fruit	_____	_____

23. Now I'd like to get your impression of some of the other stores in this area. Here is a list of some of them.

   1. Which of these stores have you ever shopped in? (Write names in column 1).
   2. How would you rank these stores to each other in overall prices - for <u>goods</u> <u>of equal quality</u>? (Record 1- for lowest, 2- for next lowest, etc. in column 2).
   3. How would you say their overall prices compare to the prices of the supermarkets? (Ask for each small store separately).

      a. Is _____ lower in overall prices for <u>goods</u> of <u>equal quality</u> than the lowest supermarket? (If no, go to next question. If yes, record "lower" in column 3).

      b. Is it higher than the highest supermarket? (If no, go to next question. If yes, record "higher" in column 3).

      c. If "no" to both a & b, between which two supermarkets do you think its prices would fall? (Record lower, higher, or names of the two stores in column 3).

   4. Now let's consider quality of goods at these small stores. First quality of fresh meat. What is your impression of the quality of fresh meat at each store-- ignoring price. (Record number in column 4).

	Prices			Quality	
(1) Store	(2) Rank Small Only	(3) vs. Large	(4) Fresh Meat	(5) Fresh Produce
_____	_____	_____	_____	_____
_____	_____	_____	_____	_____
_____	_____	_____	_____	_____
_____	_____	_____	_____	_____
_____	_____	_____	_____	_____

24. I'd like to ask you some questions about prices charged by different kinds
    of stores - just give the answer that comes to your mind first, - very quickly.
    What kind of prices is each of the following stores likely to charge -
    (1) high, (2) average, or (3) low?

    a. A new store? _____

    b. A store in a large shopping center? _____

    c. A small store? _____

    d. A store with an expensive interior? _____

    e. A store that advertises a lot? _____

    f. A store that gives trading stamps? _____

    g. A store that is untidy? _____

    h. A store that stays open very late? _____

    i. A store that offers a wide assortment? _____

    j. A store that offers lots of extra services? _____

    k. A store that offers many come-ons (loss leaders) is
       likely to be _____ on its other prices?

25. Which of these three things would you guess costs a food store most? _____
    (1) advertising, (2) interior fixtures, or (3) trading stamps?____ _____
    Least? _____
    How do you believe food prices are affected by a store's ad-
    vertising costs? Made higher (1) _____, made lower (2) _____
    not affected (3) _____
    How do you believe food prices are affected by a store's costs
    for trading stamps? Made higher (1) _____, made lower (2) _____
    not affected (3) _____
    How do you believe food prices are affected by a store's
    costs for expensive, modern fixtures? Made higher (1) _____
    made lower (2) _____, not affected (3) _____.

26. Do you save trading stamps? Yes (1) _____, No (2) _____
    If yes, approximately how many books did you save last
    year? 1 - 3 (1) _____, 4 - 6 (2) _____, over 6 (3) _____

27. Sex: **Male** _____   Female _____

28. Which of your neighbors do you talk to most? _____.
    Where does she live? _____
    Do you discuss food stores and food values with her?   _____
    Yes (1) _____, No (2) _____

29. Marital status: Married (1) _____, Single (2) _____   _____

30. Size of household _____   _____

31. Number of children _____   _____
    Ages of children _____   _____

32. Working status: Housewife (1) _____, Full time employee (2) _____   _____
    Part time employee (3) _____.
    If part time employee, average number of hours worked   _____
    per week _____

33. How long have you lived in this neighborhood? _____   _____

34. Highest grade completed in school _____   _____

35. Age class _____   _____

36. Income class _____   _____

37. Do you usually shop by auto? Yes (1) _____, No (2) _____   _____

INTERVIEWER INSTRUCTIONS

This consumer interview is concerned mainly with opinions and impressions.

We don't care whether the shopper knows what prices are at a certain
store, or how that store compares to another for a specific product.
All we want is her impression, or what she would guess. It doesn't
matter if she has ever been in the store, we still want her impression.
She could get her impression by shopping at the store, just riding or
walking past, reading the store's ads, talking to friends, or any other
way. Her impressions may have been formed in these or other ways, but
she does have impressions and it is the resulting impression that we
want.

Carry a copy of the newspaper story with you -- it helps to secure
cooperation.

COVER SHEET:

The person to be interviewed is the person who does most of the shopping
for the family. But we are only interested in those shoppers who shop
in the area defined on the cover sheet for most of their shopping. The
questions on the cover are intended to screen so that you can quickly
determine whether or not the person you're talking to should be interviewed.

Even if it turns out that the person you're talking to is not the shopper,
or even if no one answers, make a record of the address, date, time of
day, and the result. Under result enter any information that may make
it easier to establish contact -- is the dwelling **unit** vacant? Is the
family on vacation? Is there no answer because the wife works? etc.

PAGE ONE

Questions 1 - 5   Tell the respondent the alternatives. If she asks
                     how to make the comparison, just say, "Compared to
                     most people in this area." If she gives an answer
                     not covered by the suggested alternatives, write it
                     in on the right

Questions 6 - 10   These questions refer to the respondent's usual
                     pattern of shopping.
                     Do not ask for or accept answers for last week.
                     The question on fill-ins refers to trips made
                     for items like milk, soap, or bread and stops
                     made when out for purposes other than food
                     shopping.

PAGE TWO:

Question 11   The purpose of this question is to find out when the
                major shopping trip is made -- day and time of day.

Questions 12-14   These questions are concerned with the respondent's
                shopping habits. Do NOT mention the categories
                given!

                Question twelve has its object to determine where
                shopping is usually done for the major shopping trip.
                Even if "yes" is the first answer probe to find out
                if a second store is used. Do NOT mention categories
                given!
                12A Record the store named first and record the
                reasons for selection. If the reasons do not fit
                into the category given enter them under 'Other (10)'.
                Do this even when some reasons are given that fit
                and others which do not.

                12B Record the name of the store given second, and
                then proceed as in 12A.

                13 Record the name of the store where meat shopping
                is done. Do this even if the store name given is
                not one of those on your lists. If it is unfamiliar
                to you, ask the address. Then proceed as in 12A.

                14 Record as in 13, except this question is for
                produce. If the respondent asks for clarification,
                explain that produce are fresh fruits and vegetables--
                lettuce, carrots, bananas, etc.

PAGE THREE

Question 15   This question is for fill-in shopping only -- it is
                divided into that done when all stores are open and
                that done when the large super-markets are closed.

Question 16   This question is trying to determine which stores the
                respondent would not shop in, and why she would not.
                Record the store name and the reason.

Question 17   This is a most important question! For the study to
                be a success and for the questionnaire to be used
                ALL FOUR blanks must be filled in -- no duplications
                must exist. The respondent is to consider overall
                prices and prices for goods of equal quality.
                Enter only one store in each blank. If two are named,
                ask "which would you pick if you had to name one."

Question 18-19   These questions seek information about the last
                  shopping trip made by the respondent. It is
                  possible that the last major order did not
                  include either a meat or produce purchase.
                  When this is the case ask about the last purchase
                  of fresh meat (or fresh produce) and note on the
                  form that the purchase was not a part of the last
                  major order.

PAGE FOUR:

Question 20   This is the most crucial question in the interview!

                  1. Hand the respondent the list of items. Record
                      those that are important in her <u>food store</u>
                      buying. This means that milk, eggs, and bread
                      delivered to the home are not to be included.

                      Five items must be included for the interview
                      to be fully utilized. Even if these items
                      were purchased at stores other than those used
                      on her last major shopping trip, get the infor-
                      mation on five items. If these items are not
                      among the items she considers most important --
                      point out that you would like her to select
                      five from the list.

                  2. Note that this question asks the brand and
                      size bought most often of the five items
                      selected from the list. It does not refer
                      to her last shopping trip. Obviously, items
                      like ground beef, lettuce, eggs, <u>etc.</u> are not
                      branded; however, sized do vary in lettuce, cuts
                      do differ in steak, ground beef does have
                      different quality levels, eggs are graded and
                      sized. It is this sort of information that is
                      to be entered in column two for normally un-
                      branded items.

                  3. Record the store at which the item is usually
                      purchased.

Question 4-6   All refer to prices at the usual store for that item/
                  and to prices during the preceding two to three weeks.
                  A single number is desired in each case.

                  4. Is the usual or most frequent price and does not
                      not include specials. If the store almost always
                      offers the item at a particular price, but labels
                      it as "special", that price is the "usual" price.

5-6. Are the lowest and highest prices during this
two to three week period. Either one or both
could be the same as the "usual" price.

7. All 3 parts refer to changes in prices.
   a. Refers to a fairly long period - tell the
      respondent the categories.
   b. Refers to the past 3 weeks. Record either
      0 for no changes. 1-2 for one or two changes,
      or 2+ for more than two changes. The answer
      can be 0 only if 4, 5, and 6 are the same-
      check consistency, and ask respondent further
      questions to get consistency if required.
   c. Refers to the difference between the price
      before the change and the price after the
      change. Record in cents.

8. This question asks the respondent to compare
   prices of the supermarkets for the named item
   on the typical day-ignoring specials. Record
   the answer.

PAGE FIVE:

Questions 21 & 22   The idea of this question is to get the respondent
                     to give his impression of the different quality
                     levels of meat and produce in each of the large
                     super-markets.
                     Enter the number (1 - above average, 2 - average,
                     3 - below average) that corresponds to the re-
                     spondent's answer. If the respondent should balk
                     at giving the answer because she's never shopped
                     the store, remind her that it's her impressions
                     that are wanted. If this won't work ask her to
                     guess, or ask her to give her opinion and say
                     that if she's not sure, you'll mark the response
                     that way.

Question 23   This is somewhat similar to question 17, except
                     that this time the respondent's impressions of
                     prices in the smaller stores in the area is
                     being sought. First, show her the list of small
                     stores. Then enter in column one the stores she
                     has shopped. If she has not shopped in any of
                     the stores on the list, ask which small stores she ·
                     has shopped in-enter the names of those in column
                     one.

2. If only one small store is used, no answer
can be given in column two. Otherwise ask her to
rank them in overall prices: 1 for the lowest,
2 for the next lowest, etc.
3. a. Is the small store named lower in price
        than the lowest priced supermarket? If
        yes, enter "lower". If no, proceed
        to b.
   b. Is the small store named higher in price
        than the highest priced supermarket? If
        yes, enter "higher". If no proceed to c.
   c. Is to be used only if both a & b have been
        answered 'No' and indicates that the
        respondent sees the small store currently
        being asked about as competitive with the
        large supers. If she sees it this way,
        enter the names of the two stores between
        which she feels this particular small
        store's prices fall.

4.& 5. Are the counterpart for the small stores
        of questions 21 & 22 for the large stores.
        They are to be answered with a number
        (1 - above average, 2 - average, 3 - below
        average) that corresponds to the answer
        given.

Question 24-37   These are largely straight forward and self-explanatory.

Among those which have had slight problems
are:
24.g. Occassionally the respondent will say
        she doesn't know because she wouldn't
        shop in an untidy store--this is not
        what was asked. She was asked if a
        store were untidy, what would its
        prices be like! Point this out
        politely to her.

24.k. This asks about the prices of other
        items when a store uses loss leaders-
        specials that are used to attract
        patronage and may be sold at cost or
        lower.

PAGE SEVEN:

25.   The respondent is not expect to <u>know</u>
        the answer to this question. We want
        her to guess - a "don't know" is in-
        appropriate since we aren't asking
        what she knows.

26. Tell the respondent the alternatives available if she has difficulty.

27. Normally, it would seem that this question need not be asked.

28. The name and address of the neighbor is desired so we can compare the answers given by people who talk together. Tell her "We're curious as to whether people who talk together have the same impression."

29. If divorced or widowed, write in on right.

33. The neighborhood is the one in which the stores we are studying are the nearest food stores.

34. Highest grade is to be expressed in years. If the respondent has gone beyond high school, enter her exact words.

35&36. Normally the respondent will have no reservation about this information if you simply hand her the card asking "Would you please tell me which letter applies to your age group" or "Would you please tell me which letter is appropriate for your family income.

Appendix C.

STORE SAMPLE

In-store shelf pricing was performed in every supermarket within the five neighborhoods and most of the small food stores. A total of 29 supermarkets and 36 small stores were studied, divided according to the list below. The line of demarcation between supermarkets and small stores was 5000 square feet of selling space.

Community	Supermarkets	Small Stores
Greensboro	6	8
Havertown	6	6
New York	4	6
St. Louis	6	9
San Francisco	7	7
TOTAL	29	36

Appendix D.

CALCULATION OF
MARKET BASKET PRICE INDICES

The market basket index for each store was calculated as a weighted average of relatives. A separate relative was computed for each store for each item, using the neighborhood mean price as the base for the relative. Weights were applied at two different stages as shown by the equation below.

$$\text{Index}_L = \frac{\sum\limits_{j}\left(W_j \dfrac{\sum\limits_{i}\left(W_i \dfrac{P_{iL}}{\bar{P}_i}\right)}{\sum\limits_{i} W_i}\right)}{\sum\limits_{j} W_j}$$

L = Store number

i = Item number

j = Product category number

P_{iL} = Price for item i at store L

$\bar{P}_i$ = Mean price for item i within neighborhood

$$\bar{P}_i = \frac{\sum\limits_{L=1}^{N} P_{iL}}{N} \; ; \qquad N = \text{Number of supermarkets within neighborhood}$$

W = Weight

The weights were determined by the Bureau of Labor Statistics for the individual communities by a survey of consumer expenditures in 1962. (Durham figures were used for Greensboro; and Philadelphia figures, for Havertown. The other three cities in the study were in the BLS survey.)

Weights were introduced at both the individual item stage and the product category stage. This two-stage weighting was employed because some product categories were sampled more heavily than others.

In some instances more than one brand/size was used for a specific item; e.g., Crisco Shortening (48 oz.) and Wesson Liquid Shortening (pt.). Separate relatives were computed for each brand/size and the unweighted mean was used as the item relative. The items within each product category are listed below.

Product Category	*Items*
Cereal	Corn Flakes
	Corn Meal
	Flour
	Oats
	Rice
Bakery	Bread
	Cookies
	Crackers
Dairy	Butter
	Cheese
	Evaporated Milk
	Ice Cream
	Milk
Sugar and Sweet	Corn Syrup
	Gelatin
	Jelly
	Sugar
Processed Food	Corn
	Dried Beans
	Fish (Frozen)
	Fruit Cocktail
	Green Beans
	Green Beans (Frozen)
	Orange Juice
	Orange Juice (Frozen)

Product Category (Continued)	*Items* (Continued)
Processed Food (Continued)	Peaches
	Peas
	Peas (Frozen)
	Pineapple
	Prunes
	Salmon (Canned)
	Tomatoes
	Tomato Juice
	Tuna (Canned)
Fats and Oils	Lard
	Margarine
	Peanut Butter
	Salad Dressing
	Shortening
Beverage	Coffee, Instant
	Coffee, Regular
	Cola
	Tea
Prepared	Baby Food
	Baked Beans
	Catsup
	Tomato Soup
Eggs	Eggs
Fresh Vegetables	Cabbage
	Carrots
	Celery
	Green Beans
	Lettuce
	Onions
	Potatoes, White
	Spinach
	Sweet Potatoes
	Tomatoes
Fresh Fruit	Apples
	Bananas
	Lemons
	Oranges
Beef and Veal	Chuck Roast
	Ground Beef
	Rib Roast
	Steak
	Veal Cutlet

Product Category (Continued)	_Items_ (Continued)
Pork	Bacon
	Pork Chops
Other Meat	Canned
	Frankfurters
	Leg of Lamb
Poultry	Chicken
Non-Food	Cleaning Tissues
	Detergent
	Toilet Tissue

Within each neighborhood, a precise brand and size was specified for each item; e.g., Carnation Evaporated Milk (14½ oz.), Kellogg's Corn Flakes (12 oz.), Center Cut Loin Pork Chops (lb.), and Del Monte Yellow Cling Heavy Syrup Canned Peaches (29 oz.).

If a particular item within a product category was not available, the summation with respect to sub-script "i" simply covered fewer items. The relative computed for the product category still received the weight ascertained by the BLS as appropriate for that category.

An index of 100 (or 1.00) means that the store on the average had prices equal to the mean for the supermarkets in the neighborhood. Small stores are excluded from this mean, although indices are of course computed for small stores as well as supermarkets. Indices above 100 indicate stores with prices higher on the average, and indices below 100 indicate stores lower on the average.

Price indices for the different departments were computed in precisely the same way. The only difference being that fewer product categories were involved for any particular department.

STORE SERVICES
AND RETAILER QUESTIONNAIRE

The local project supervisor inspected each store and interviewed each store manager. (Results in New York were too limited to permit their inclusion.) The retailer questionnaire was similar to the consumer questionnaire in many respects, but it also covered certain aspects of store operations and policies.

Higher costs of operation were hypothesized as associated with higher price levels, both for perceived prices and for reality prices. It was, therefore, necessary to establish at least a crude measure of operating costs. Perceived quality of fresh food and the offering of extra services were employed as possible indicators of higher costs.

Consumers were asked their perceptions of fresh meat and fresh produce quality levels for the various stores. The mean rating per respondent was accepted as the perceived quality level, with equal weight given to meat and produce.

The determination of a "service" level for each store was filled with difficulties and assumptions. Should we simply count the number of services offered? Surely services differ in their cost to the stores—and also in their importance to the consumer. Any count of the number of services ignores these differences as well as ignoring the quality of performance for the service. We recognized these problems but compromised on a count as a first approximation—to do much more would require a separate research project on the measurement of service levels.

The next task was the definition of a service. What should be counted? Is free parking a service? How about extra long hours? Any answers to these questions are arbitrary. Our basic assumption is that a service oriented store will score high on a count approach regardless of the list of services employed and a limited service store will score low—provided the list is established before starting the data collection process. The measurements are not precise, but the method should not introduce bias.

The following services constitute the list employed for the project: music, air conditioning, express lines, charge accounts, parcel pick-up stations, boys to carry packages, telephone orders, home delivery, check cashing, clerks for weighing fresh produce, fresh meat department, fresh fish department, bakery department, fresh produce department, delicatessen department, and any additional services or departments that the local project supervisor thought should be included. The last item posed certain hazards, but they were minimized since all comparisons were within the same neighborhood—with the supervisor held constant for all stores compared. When this technique was applied, some store managers wished to add other services such as honor bottle return. Other managers seemed to stress the number of check-outs as a sign of service. The actual analysis used only the listed services with no modifications by the project supervisor.

Number of services and perceived quality were tested separately against perceived price, using rank correlation. They were also tested against reality price (as measured by the market basket index). The results (page 49, Table 6) show positive association between perceived price and either service or perceived quality in every community.

RETAILER INTERVIEW

1. What do you think is the main thing most customers look
    for in deciding which food store to shop in?

2. How long has this store been open?_____

3. How long have you been in the food store business?_____
    How long have you been working in this particular store?_____
    When did you first become a store manager?_____

4. Here is a list of supermarkets in the area. Which of these do
    you consider your chief competition?_____

5. Considering only goods of equal quality, which one of these
    stores has the lowest overall prices?_____
    The next lowest?_____. Which one has the highest
    overall prices - for goods of equal quality?_____
    The next highest?_____. How much
    difference do you think there would be between the highest
    priced store and the lowest priced store on an order of
    approximately $25?_____.

6. Which of these stores do you think has the lowest prices for fresh
    meat - for meat of equal quality?_____. Which store has
    the highest prices?_____. Which store has the lowest
    prices for fresh produce?_____. The highest prices?_____

7. Here is a list of some of the smaller stores in the area. Which
    of these do you consider your chief competition?_____

8. How would you rank these small stores in overall prices - for goods
    of equal quality? (1 - for lowest, etc.)

9. Where would you place these small stores in overall prices compared
    to the supermarkets?

Store	Rank	Compared to Supers
_____	____	_____
_____	____	_____
_____	____	_____
_____	____	_____
_____	____	_____
_____	____	_____

(Enter higher, lower, or names of supers between which each
 small store falls).

10. Here is a list of twelve items; how frequently would you say the price of
    each item changes at your store? (Enter 1 - for several times a month,
    2 - about once a month, 3- every few months, 4 - very rarely).

    When its price is changed, what would be a typical amount for the price
    change? (Record in cents).

Item	Frequency	Amount
Milk (½ gal).	_____	_____
Eggs (doz.)	_____	_____
Lettuce (head)	_____	_____
Steak (1 lb.)	_____	_____
Ground beef (1 lb.)	_____	_____
Bananas (1 lb.)	_____	_____
Frozen Peas (reg.)	_____	_____
Sugar (5 lb.)	_____	_____
Instant Coffee (10 oz.)	_____	_____
Paper Towels	_____	_____
Bread (loaf)	_____	_____
Canned Fruit Punch	_____	_____

11. Consumers in our survey are being asked a series of questions concerning their opinions of prices charged by different <u>types</u> of stores. They are asked to say whether they think prices would be high, average, or low for different types of stores. I'd like you to guess the answers you think the consumers will give and also indicate whether you think their answers are right. The types of stores they are being asked about are:

	Consumers	Retailer
a new store	___	___
a store in a large shopping center	___	___
a small store	___	___
a store with an expensive interior	___	___
a store that advertises a lot	___	___
a store that gives trading stamps	___	___
a store that is untidy	___	___
a store that stays open very late	___	___
a store that offers a wide assortment	___	___
a store that offers lots of extra services	___	___
a store that offers many come-ons (loss leaders) is likely to be (what) on its other prices	___	___

12. What forms of mass media advertising do you use? how often?

13. What was the strongest promotion run by a competitor during the past few months?

    How much do you think it hurt your business?

    How many customers that shift in response to such promotions do you think are lost as regular customers to you?

14. What kinds of promotions have been most successful for you (at this store)?

15. Customers frequently shift from one store to another
    or divide their patronage. From which stores do you
    think you have been gaining recently?

    What do you think is the principal reason(s)?

16. To whom might you have been losing customers recently?_____
    What might have caused this?

17. How often do you (or someone within this store) check your
    competitors' operations or shelf prices?_____
    Do you read their ads?_____Which stores?_____
    Do you report the results of your checking to anyone?

    Does anyone else in your organization check the activities
    of competitors?
    Do they ever pass information on to you about these
    activities? _____How?

18. On what items and under what circumstances are you
    permitted to change prices?

    Must you clear it first?_____with whom?_____

19. What percentage of your customers do you think are
    relatively well informed on prices of advertised specials?_____
    on shelf prices?_____

20. What are your store hours?_____

21. Which of the following services do you offer? Music_____,
    Air conditioning_____, express lines_____, charge accounts____,
    parcel pick-up stations for loading_____, boys to carry
    parcels to cars_____, telephone orders_____, home
    delivery_____, check cashing_____, clerks for weighing
    and packaging produce_____, any other special services
    _____

22. Which of the following departments do you have? Fresh
    meat____, Fresh fish_____, Fresh produce_____, Bakery,
    Delicatessen_____ Other special departments_____

23. How many cars can be parked in an area convenient to
    your store?_____.   Is this sufficent to
    accommodate your peak traffic hours? _____

24. Square footage (selling space)_____
    Number of check-outs_____
    Trading stamps given_____

25. What kinds of customers do you think are particularly
    attracted to your store?

26. Would you say that your store attempts to be (1) the
    lowest, (2) below average, (3) average, (4) slightly
    above average, or (5) among the highest in prices?_____

27. How do you think your store is distinctive - compared
    with other stores in this area?

28. How would you classify the different supermarkets quality of fresh meat-
    ignoring the question of price? Use the categories (1) above average,
    (2) average, or (3) below average.

29. How would you rate the quality of fresh produce at each super - again
    ignoring the question of price?

Store	Meat Quality	Produce Quality	Store	Meat Quality	Produce Quality

30. Now how would you classify the smaller stores in quality of fresh meat-
    ignoring price?

31. How about quality of fresh produce?

32. Are there other questions concerning your operation or the operation
    of your competitors that I should have asked?

Appendix F.

CALCULATION OF
INDIVIDUAL PERCEPTUAL ACCURACY

The underlying concept and basic measurement of individual perceptual accuracy are presented on pages 31-32. The procedure presented there requires a complete ordinal ranking of stores from each respondent. Incomplete rankings require more complicated definitions and calculations.

A complete ordinal ranking was requested in only New York. In all other cities, four ranks were requested from a list of six or seven supermarkets. Even in New York, the respondents occasionally supplied fewer than four ranks—despite concerted efforts to the contrary.

The respondent's score is based upon the number of paired comparisons implicit in four ranks. In a neighborhood with six stores, 14 paired comparisons are implicit in four ranks—each comparison except that involving the two unranked stores. Table F-1 illustrates the calculations, both for respondents who give four ranks and those who do not.

The first two respondents supplied the four ranks requested. Their perceptual accuracy scores are computed from the errors in the 14 paired comparisons. For respondent I, no errors—score .000. For respondent II, the score is equal to the mean error per comparison (based on 14). Notice the scores for both respondents are based on 14 comparisons but not the same 14.

The third respondent supplied only three ranks, yielding only 12 not 14 comparisons. Only one of these comparisons was incorrect (E versus F). It would be improper to ignore the remaining comparisons. The procedure penalizes the respondent by the expected result of random selection. First, it assumes that chance would dictate which two of the remaining three comparisons she would have made had she completed the task. Second, it assumes that chance would yield the correct answer for any comparison made half the time. The adjustment factor is thus 1/3 (1/2 of 2/3). The score is then reduced to a mean per comparison.

TABLE F-1
CALCULATION OF PERCEPTUAL ACCURACY SCORES,
INCOMPLETE ORDINAL DATA[a]

		Respondents' Rankings		
Store	*Price Index*	*I*	*II*	*III*
A	.950	1		1
B	.970	2	1	2
C	.995			
D	1.010		2	
E	1.035	5	6	6
F	1.040	6	5	

[a]Scorings:

```
        Number of Possible Paired Comparisons = 15
        Number of Paired Comparisons Requested = 14
        I  Number Comparisons Made = 14
                                Incorrect          None
                                Score              .000
        II Number Comparisons Made = 14
                                Incorrect  AB      .020
                                           AD      .060
                                           CD      .015
                                           EF      .005
                                            Σ      .100
                                Score              .0071
        III Number Comparisons Made = 12
                                Incorrect  EF      .005
        Comparisons Not Made  CD   .015
                              CF   .045
                              DF   .030
                               Σ   .090
        Adjusted Penalty 2/3 × 1/2 × .090          .030
                                                   .035
                                Score              .0025
```

Appendix G.

CONSUMER VARIABLES TESTED FOR RELATIONSHIP TO PERCEPTUAL ACCURACY

Twenty-four different consumer characteristics were tested as explanatory variables for perceptual accuracy (see Appendix F). Multiple regression was the basic approach used, but several variables had to be transformed first.

Two general problems existed. (1) Several explanatory variables were dichotomous or trichotomous. This posed limited difficulty, and the dummy variable technique was used for these variables (see the list below in order to identify the specific variables). (2) Other explanatory variables were not independent. Factor analysis revealed which variables

TABLE G-1
MERGING OF VARIABLES: ILLUSTRATIVE DATA

Category	I Compare Advertised Prices	
	Cumulative Percentage	Mid-point
a. Hardly Ever	20	10.0
b. Sometimes	70	45.0
c. Usually	100	85.0

Category	II Look Hard for Low Price	
	Cumulative Percentage	Mid-point
a. Not as hard as others	15	7.5
b. About the same	65	40.0
c. Harder	100	82.5

Score Calculation

Respondent #1: Answers Ib and IIc = 45.0 + 82.5 = 127.5
Respondent #2: Answers Ia and IIa = 10.0 + 7.5 = 17.5
Respondent #3: Answers Ic and IIc = 85.0 + 82.5 = 167.5

164

had high loadings on the same factor. These variables were merged into a single variable (see the list below for the variables merged).

The criterion for merging was a loading of .40 or more on the same factor in at least four of the five neighborhoods. This cut-off was used with a factor analysis based on seven factors.

The merging of variables is illustrated in Table G-1. The mid-point of the cumulative frequency was calculated for each category of each variable to be merged. The respondent's score is equal to the sum of the scores corresponding to her answers. (Means could be used as well, but neither R^2 nor the regressions signs would be affected.)

The original variables, type of transformation, and classification are listed in Table G-2. Two types of classifications were employed: (1) general factors that contribute to better performance in any undertaking—motivation, experience, effort, or general ability; and (2) factors more directly related to shopping—shopping behavior, shopping attitude, or socio-economic characteristics. Some variables were not assigned to any performance category because that classification system was inappropriate for them. In other cases assignment was somewhat arbitrary, but it was reinforced by the factor analyses and substantive results.

The regression equations are discussed in Appendix H.

TABLE G-2
TRANSFORMATION OF CONSUMER VARIABLES AND THEIR ASSIGNMENT TO CATEGORIES

No. in Questionnaire	No. in Analysis	Variable	Transformation[a]	Performance Factor[b]	Shopping Classification[c]
1	1	Enjoyment	Merge with 2 & 3	Motivation/Effort	Attitude
2		Effort	Merge with 1 & 3		
3		Satisfaction	Merge with 1 & 2		
4	2, 3	Self-evaluation	Dummy[d]	—[e]	Attitude
5	4	Look for Price	Merge with 7 & 8	Motivation/Effort	Behavior
6	5, 6	Use of List	Dummy[d]	Effort	Behavior
7		Read Ads	Merge with 5 & 8		
8		Compare Adv. Prices	Merge with 5 & 7		
9	7	Shopping Frequency	None	Experience	Behavior
10	8	Evaluation of Others	Dummy	—[e]	Attitude
12A	9	Price-Reason for Store Selection	Dummy	Effort	Attitude
12B	10	More than One Regular Store	Dummy	Experience	Behavior
18	11	Order Size	Merge with 30 & 31	Motivation/Experience	Behavior[f]
27	12	Sex	Dummy	—[e]	Socio-econ
28	13	Discuss Food Shopping	Dummy	Motivation	Behavior

29	Marital Status	Dummy	——[e]	Socio-econ
30	Household Size	Merge with 18 & 31		Socio-econ
31	No. of Children	Merge with 18 & 30		Socio-econ
32	Employment Status	Dummy[d]	Motivation	Socio-econ
33	Time in Neighborhood (Tenure)	Merge with 35	Experience/Gen. Abilities	Socio-econ
34	Education	None	Gen. Abilities	Socio-econ
35	Age	Merge with 33		Socio-econ
36	Income	None	Motivation/Gen. Abilities	Socio-econ
37	Auto Use in Shopping	Dummy	Experience	Behavior

[a]The transformations are discussed in the text within this Appendix.

[b]Four factors contributing to performance are employed: motivation, effort, experience, and general abilities. Some variables are classified in two categories while others are not assigned to any category within this classification system. The results of tests using this system are on page 73.

[c]Three shopping classification categories are employed: shopping attitude, shopping behavior, and socio-economic characteristics. All variables are assigned to one and only one category. The results of tests using this system are on page 74.

[d]Trichotomous question resulting in two dummy variables.

[e]Not assigned to any performance factor.

[f]Questions 18, 30, and 31 have heavy loadings on the same factor. Household size and number of children would seem socio-economic variables while order size is shopping behavior. The merged variable is assigned to the behavior category since it seems to reflect the effect of the socio-economic variables on food shopping rather than the initial variables.

Appendix H.

MULTIPLE REGRESSION EQUATIONS FOR TESTING CONSUMER VARIABLES

Linear multiple regression was employed to test for relationships between individual perceptual accuracy and consumer characteristics. Two separate equations were calculated in each community. The first used a step-wise regression routine (BMD-02R) which accepted additional variables as long as the F ratio for the new variable was significant at the .05 level, and the second employed all 20 variables (after transformations and as presented in column 2 of Table G-2).

The first and shorter equation was used to determine the strength of the relationship between the independent variables and perceptual accuracy and to identify the most important explanatory variables. Resulting R^2 values and the variables entering the equations are presented in Table H-1 for each community.

The second equation was used to test whether the direction of relationship between perceptual accuracy and the specific variables was consistent. The test for consistency used the signs of the regression

TABLE H-1
STEP-WISE REGRESSION RESULTS FOR EACH COMMUNITY

	Greensboro	Havertown	New York	St. Louis	San Francisco
R^2	.12	.05	.04	.07	.05
Variables in Equation	Usually Use List	Usually Use List	Education	Usually Use List	Store Selected for Price
	Sometimes Use List	Store Selected for Price		Shop More than One Store	Age/Tenure
	Frequency of Shopping	Shop More than One Store		Age/Tenure	
	Age/Tenure				

coefficients, compared to a random distribution of half positive and half negative signs. The theoretical model was $(\frac{1}{2} + \frac{1}{2})^5$ for each variable since there were five observations—one in each community.

TABLE H-2
CONSISTENCY OF REGRESSION COEFFICIENT
SIGNS FOR TWENTY CONSUMER VARIABLES

Variable	No. of Similar Signs	Modal Relation
Socio-economic		
Income	5	Positive
Full-time Employment	5	Positive
Part-time Employment	4	Positive
Male	4	Positive
Single	4	Positive
Age/Tenure	4	Positive
Education	3	Inverse
Shopping Attitudes		
Price As Reason for Store Selection	5	Positive
Believe Others Good Shoppers	4	Inverse
Believe Self Good Shopper	4	Inverse
Believe Self Average	3	Positive
General Atittude[a]	3	Positive
Shopping Behavior		
Order/Household Size[b]	4	Positive
Auto Use in Shopping	4	Positive
Search Effort	3	Positive
Frequency of Shopping	3	Positive
Discuss Shopping	3	Positive
Usual Use of List	3	Positive
Shop More Than One Store	3	Inverse
Sometime Use List	3	Inverse

[a]Merged variable based on enjoyment, satisfaction, and thought input.

[b]Merged variable based on order size, household size, and number of children.

Four or five of the neighborhoods would have the same sign for any specific variable (under the null hypothesis) with probability equal to 3/8. The expected number of variables within any particular category (meeting the four or five out of five criterion) is then 3/8 times the number of variables within the category. The comparisons are shown in Table 6 of page 74.

Statistical tests for the consistency of signs for variables within any category require calculation of exact probabilities from the binomial. The appropriate expression is $(3/8 + 5/8)^n$ where n is equal to the number of variables within a particular category. As seen below, the socio-economic variables show very consistent behavior; but the two shopping categories are not significantly different from random results under the null hypothesis.

Category	Observed No.	Probability of Observed or More
Socio-economic	6 of 7	.01
Shopping Attitude	3 of 5	.28
Shopping Behavior	2 of 8	.63

The number of neighborhoods in which each variable has the same sign and the modal direction of relationship are presented in Table H–2.

Multiple coefficients of determination (R^2) for the complete equations with 20 independent variables were Greensboro .19, New York .13, St. Louis .12, San Francisco .09, and Havertown .08.

INDEX

INDEX